ADVANCE PRAISE FOR *THIS WILD LAND*

"Eighteen years ago, Andrew Vietze did something many people dream of but few of us have the guts to do; he left a prestigious office job to take an entry-level position working in the Maine North Woods. *This Wild Land* records his adventures and misadventures as a ranger at Baxter State Park: home to legendary Katahdin, beloved by both Henry David Thoreau and Teddy Roosevelt, and arguably the last wild place in the Eastern United States. Vietze's story is at once inspirational, frankly heartfelt, and endlessly entertaining. In other words, it has all the makings of a new Maine classic."

—PAUL DOIRON, author of *The Poacher's Son* and *Dead by Dawn*

"When young people ask for advice about becoming a writer, my response is generally as follows: write (and read) all the time. *And get a real job.* Usually, I recommend plumbing, because it's lucrative and also because there are always good stories to be found in kitchens and bathrooms. . . . Having read Vietze's fine storytelling, I think I might recommend his path instead. Beginning as a magazine writer, Vietze found a real, and really wonderful, job, patrolling and protecting Baxter State Park. One of the most beautiful places on earth, Baxter also boasts Katahdin, the highest mountain in Maine and the northern terminus of the Appalachian Trail. The work of a Baxter ranger is varied, challenging and sometimes life-saving . . . and has provided Andrew Vietze with an abundance of good stories. He offers these with humor, verve, an eye for the telling detail and an infectious delight in this rugged corner of the natural world, and its human and non-human inhabitants."

—KATE BRAESTRUP, *New York Times* bestselling author of *Here if You Need Me*

"The experience of reading *This Wild Land*, floating in the eddies of Andrew Vietze's profoundly captivating and elegantly unpretentious prose—seeing through his eyes the natural world's quiet beauty and ruthless tragedy—offers an ideal escape from the unrelenting madness of modern life. Only an observant, gifted writer who has spent eighteen years working beneath the foreboding summit of Katahdin could achieve the humility to write such a perfect tribute to the magnificent park in the middle of Maine."

—MICHAEL FINKEL, *New York Times* bestselling author of *The Stranger in the Woods*

THIS WILD LAND

Two Decades of Adventure as a Park Ranger
in the Shadow of Katahdin

ANDREW VIETZE

Appalachian Mountain Club Books
Boston, Massachusetts

AMC is a nonprofit organization, and sales of AMC Books fund our mission of protecting the Northeast outdoors. If you appreciate our efforts and would like to become a member or make a donation to AMC, visit outdoors.org, call 800-372-1758, or contact us at Appalachian Mountain Club, 10 City Square, Boston, MA 02129.

outdoors.org/books-maps

Front cover photographs © Appalachian Mountain Club or via unsplash.com
Back cover photograph by Lisa Mossel Vietze
Map by Ken Dumas © Appalachian Mountain Club
Cover design by Jon Lavalley
Interior design by Eric Edstam

Library of Congress Cataloging-in-Publication data

Names: Vietze, Andrew, author.
Title: This wild land : two decades of adventure as a park ranger in the shadow of Katahdin / Andrew Vietze.
Description: Boston, MA : Appalachian Mountain Club Books, [2021] | Summary: "A memoir from a long-time ranger at Baxter State Park in Maine"-- Provided by publisher.
Identifiers: LCCN 2021043357 (print) | LCCN 2021043358 (ebook) | ISBN 9781628421323 (trade paperback) | ISBN 9781628421330 (epub) | ISBN 9781628421347 (mobi)
Subjects: LCSH: Vietze, Andrew. | Park rangers--Maine--Baxter--Biography. | Wilderness areas--Maine--Baxter State Park.
Classification: LCC SB481.6.V54 A3 2021 (print) | LCC SB481.6.V54 (ebook) | DDC 363.6/8092 [B]--dc23
LC record available at https://lccn.loc.gov/2021043357
LC ebook record available at https://lccn.loc.gov/2021043358

The paper used in this publication meets the minimum requirements of the American National Standard for Information Sciences-Permanence of Paper for Printed Library Materials, ANSI Z39.48-1984. ∞

Outdoor recreation activities by their very nature are potentially hazardous. This book is not a substitute for good personal judgment and training in outdoor skills. Due to changes in conditions, use of the information in this book is at the sole risk of the user. The author and the Appalachian Mountain Club assume no liability for accidents happening to, or injuries sustained by, readers who engage in the activities described in this book.

Interior pages and cover are printed on responsibly harvested paper stock certified by The Forest Stewardship Council®, an independent auditor of responsible forestry practices.

FSC

www.fsc.org

MIX

Paper from responsible sources

FSC® C005010

Printed in the United States of America, using vegetable-based inks.

5 4 3 2 1   21 22 23 24 25 26

BAXTER STATE PARK

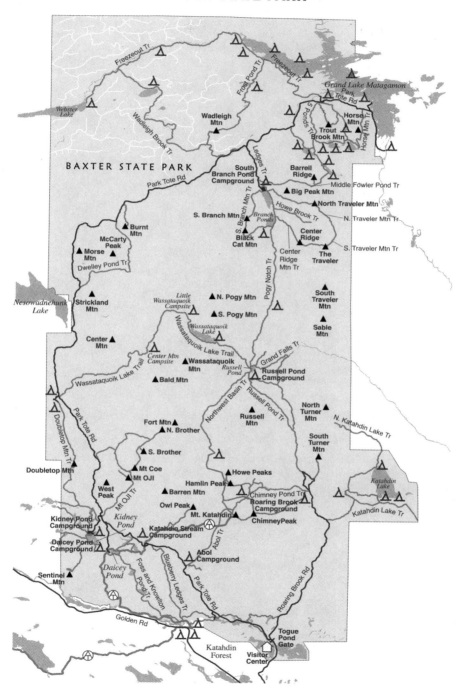

CONTENTS

INTRODUCTION

Rangers like to tell stories. Yarning, cracking each other up in the station under the glow of the gas light, sharing tales of past adventures while leaning on the hood of a park truck, is something of a tradition. This is especially true in a place like Maine, where fish tales and pot-belly philosophizing come with the territory. And it's certainly the case among Baxter Park rangers. I imagine it's the same everywhere. Living in a wild place, under unique circumstances, without the distractions of TVs or phones or the World Wide Web, we end up providing our own entertainment. Stories are what we do. And our visitors love when we stand beside their campfires and tell them of mishaps and mayhem in the woods that surround.

This book is a product of that.

And also the fact that Jennifer Wehunt, former editorial director of AMC Books, now with PBS's *Frontline*—of whom I'm a fan—asked me whether I'd be interested in writing about life as a ranger.

I'm no special ranger. Plenty among Baxter Park's finest are better at their jobs than I, and many have had far more and far crazier adventures—and thus better stories—than I have. (I'd love to read a book by ex–Kidney Pond ranger Dean Levasseur, for example.)

All I can do is tell my story.

Everything in here is true, and I tried to present it all as exactly as my failing memory allowed. I fill my little park-issued Maine Forest Service Smokey the Bear notebook every year with thoughts and recollections but I miss a lot, and these pages are full of stories as best I can remember them. I didn't use the real names of any park visitors for the sake of privacy. Any and all mistakes are mine.

I wrote this book during the summer of 2020—"The Year of Covid," as my partner Charity jotted in the Daicey Pond Campground guestbook to explain why there are no guest signatures under the 2020 heading. The coronavirus changed a lot about how we do our job. We kept our distance from campers, closed many public spaces, and changed our cleaning and rescue protocols, but I didn't want the pandemic to color all of these pages because it is an aberration (at least I hope it is).

One thing was for sure, as our park director pointed out at the end of the season: people needed us more than ever this year. After living in quarantine for months, everyone was desperate to get out and explore. Nothing spreads cabin fever like a lockdown virus.

I was hankering to get out, too. I imagine many Americans are actively wishing they could be back at their workplaces this year. I feel that way every year, an actual yearning to be back on the job—a deep desire to do this work—and the same is true of most of my colleagues. We are fortunate to be able to live and make a living in Governor Baxter's unique creation.

I'd like to thank Jennifer Wehunt for showing interest in my story and to thank editor Tim Mudie for making it better. I'd also like to thank all my fellow Baxter Park rangers, past and present, with whom I've had the privilege to serve. You are all a credit to the governor's vision.

Mostly, though, I'd like to express my gratitude to my two boys, Gus and Leo, my heart and my soul, for allowing me to be a park ranger. I know you've made sacrifices so that I can continue to do this job I love, and it means the world.

This is for you.

PROLOGUE

JUSTINE LOOKS LIKE A DIVER IN A JACQUES COUSTEAU SPECIAL, scrambling from one rock to the next above me, climbing into the cloud. Her headlamp refracts in the suspended water, making a bright cone in the gloom. It's 12:30 A.M. and we're on the Hunt Spur, a tangle of boulders high on the side of Katahdin, just about to crest onto the Gateway, the point where the Hunt Trail opens onto the long plateau of the Tableland. The cold October wind is already tearing at our park-issued shells, shoving us off-balance. I can only imagine what it's like ripping across the flat up above.

We reach the spot where the coordinates say we should find our guy. Justine checks the GPS again. Our headlamps barely penetrate the thick nimbostratus. We can see maybe 10 feet beyond our hands, and we've picked up no sign of any life.

The radio crackles.

"54 to 613, 615."

Ranger Bruce White, down at Katahdin Stream Ranger Station, is "54." He's the duty officer this evening, the ranking ranger in the park, and he's the one that sent me and Justine—613 and 615, respectively—up the mountain.

I fish my handheld out of my pack, turn my back to the roaring wind, and trigger the mic:

"10-3."

"Anything?"

"Negative. We're at the coordinates. I've been blowing the whistle. Nothing."

"How are the conditions?"

"It's really slick up here. The wind must be 40 miles an hour. Every time we stop, ice forms on our pants."

"All right, be careful. Let me talk to the chief, and I'll get back to you."

I bend against the gale, stuff the radio back into my pack, and turn to Justine. I have to lean in and scream for her to hear me.

"You OK?"

"I'm fine," she says, tucking her long brown hair into her knit hat.

"Let's keep moving until they tell us to stop."

———

Maine's highest peak and the terminus of the Appalachian Trail, Katahdin is unforgiving territory in the dark of night, which is why we rangers recommend that climbers make every effort to be down before the sun is.

We are still climbing, heading up in search of an Appalachian Trail thru-hiker who deployed his ResQLink personal locator beacon, otherwise known as a PLB. These GPS-based gadgets send your coordinates to a satellite, providing rescuers your location in the event you need help, kind of like OnStar for hikers.

The U.S. Air Force, the agency responsible for inland search and rescue, picked up this guy's ping and called the Maine State Police's Houlton Regional Communications Center, which in turn called Baxter Park's chief ranger, Dan Rinard. Dan is sitting in his truck in a parking lot in town so he can receive a radio relay from us and still talk on the phone to the nation's flying corps. This workaround is required because (thankfully) there is no reliable cell service in this "forever wild" wilderness. Bruce, our supervisor, my partner at my earliest duty station, one of my besties, and almost always on the same shift as me, serves as the link between us and the chief.

AT northbounders—or NOBOs—represent the fittest and best hikers in Baxter Park, having already trekked more than 2,000 miles from

Georgia to Maine with loads on their backs. Unlike many of the day-hikers who arrive to climb the mile-high mountain, often grotesquely unprepared for the rigors and climate changes on the slopes of Katahdin, NOBOs have sculpted legs and well-developed lungs by the time they reach the park. They've scaled dozens of peaks, some even higher than Katahdin, including Mount Washington in the White Mountains, as they made their way north. In Maine alone, the trail is something of a beast, going up and over countless summits, from Old Speck to the Bigelows. So when a NOBO cries for help, it gets our attention.

I'm starting to worry we're not going to find this kid.

The first coordinates we got seemed to put him over the edge of the Tableland in Witherle Ravine, a deep cleft in the side of Katahdin. No one would survive there. The corrected set showed him at the Gateway, which is where Justine and I are now looking. *If I were up here,* I think, *I'd tuck right under the lip of the great plateau, out of the wind.* Justine and I decide she'll stay on the white blazes that indicate the trail, and I'll clamber off to each side to see what I can find.

A native of New Jersey, Justine Rumaker is in her late 20s and vacationed in the park as a kid, falling in love with the outdoors. When I first met her a few years ago, she wanted to be in law enforcement, like her older brother, a state trooper back home. Back then, she was just getting started at the park as a summer intern in the info/education department, fresh out of the University of Delaware. Now, like me, she's a seasoned frontcountry ranger. This is her third year at Katahdin Stream, and we've worked on several projects together: roofing an outbuilding, constructing lean-tos, building a new footbridge. We paired up for one big rescue before this one, back in July when a couple fell from a bridge onto the boulders of Katahdin Stream, and there are few other rangers I'd take over her up here with me.

I realize as I stumble around in the dark that these are similar conditions to the ones that led to the first officially recorded fatality in Baxter State Park, which also took the life of the only ranger to die in the line of duty: October storm, above treeline, late night, hiker off-trail. Of course,

Ranger Ralph Heath was climbing on the headwall that looms over Chimney Pond in a genuine blizzard on that fateful day in 1963. As cold, tired, and frustrated as we are, Justine and I are far better off than that, on the solid and wide Hunt Trail in a frozen mist.

We lost the 6-inch white blazes that mark the way a few times as we broke treeline and hauled ourselves up onto the boulders of the Hunt Spur. The trail wends around and between some enormous slabs as it leaves the last scrubby conifers, and we had a difficult time squeezing our backpacks through. To keep ourselves oriented, we started leapfrogging—Justine stood on one white blaze while I searched for the next one. It worked well, so we kept at it.

I shine my light into crevices and under crags, looking for any sort of sign, but all I find is dark and granite and more dark and granite. I blow three blasts on my rescue whistle, a 100-decibel banshee that seems as loud as a train. These search-and-rescue (SAR) staples are so ear-piercing that they're also marketed for self-defense, and every time I use it I warn Justine to put her fingers in her ears, but just like the dozens of other times I've blasted it this evening, I get no response. The wind simply swallows the sound.

I stagger back toward Justine. The fog is so thick that I can't even see her headlamp until I'm 15 feet away. It's like those stormy nights when a car's high beams are less effective than the low beams in the murk, just making the cloud glow.

The radio sparks again.

"54 to 613."

"10-3."

"The chief wants you to head up onto the Tableland and keep going to Thoreau Spring. If you don't find anything, turn around."

We push upward, still hopeful, despite the conditions. The guy has got to be out here. He could be hurt. He might be freezing. We may be his last shot.

———

When she came on duty at Katahdin Stream earlier in the day, Justine spoke with the AT hiker's mother. Apparently, the 24-year-old from Ontario, Canada, began his climb sometime after 1 P.M., well past our recommended cutoff time. Justine also learned that he was warned about making such a late start by another ranger. The kid simply shrugged. Because it's so steep, the 5.2 miles of Hunt Trail typically take climbers eight to ten hours, but AT hikers can do it much faster. Even so, there was little chance he'd be back by the time the sun set, shortly after 5. The guy also wanted to bring his own pack and was cautioned about this as well. The climb is difficult enough without carrying a load, which is why we offer thru-hikers loaner day packs. He chose to bring his own.

Justine mentioned all this to his mom, who thought the park was being too fussy. *Her* son would be fine. (We get this a lot. On busy mornings, we often stand in the parking lot at Katahdin Stream and Abol and talk to climbers about their plans, making suggestions, helping where we can. I remember the look one particular woman in her early 20s gave me when I asked her if she had more water than the single Poland Spring bottle she was carrying in her hand, on a day that was supposed to be muggy and in the 80s. She wasn't wearing a pack. "I'm good," she told me, with a smirk that said, *What do you know about me and my needs?*)

This NOBO's mom waited at the trailhead and when her son didn't return by dark, her tone did a 180, and she started to get concerned. She was upset when we initially told her we wouldn't be mounting a search. When he triggered his PLB, setting the rescue in motion, Justine went back to her to get as much information as she could—his plans, the gear he had with him, any medications . . . the standard detective work we do when planning our response. As the evening progressed, Mom grew more and more helpful.

Bruce wasn't certain we needed to go. "He had a pack, he knew what he was doing," he said to me. Bruce White has been a ranger for a long time—I often joke that he's been at the park since "after the War," but he started in the late '80s—and he had a hunch the kid would be fine. He's been working at the base of the Hunt Trail for most of his three decades at the park, and his intuition is usually right. On nights like this one, he can often tell you exactly where the hiker will hole up or estimate to within an hour what time they will be down. But a storm is pounding the summit, and the kid called for help, checking two of the biggest boxes on our "do-we-go" protocol list.

Contrary to popular belief, Baxter Park rangers don't immediately go up after every hiker who doesn't come down Katahdin. I routinely have campers run up to me to say they have seen headlamps high up on the mountain long after dark.

"Aren't you going to do something?" they ask breathlessly.

I explain that we see lights several times a week, flashing here, flashing there, like herky-jerky stars. Blinking dots on the peak are as routine as long lines at the gate in summer.

"So many people underestimate the difficulty of Katahdin," I tell them. "Unless we know of an injury, or the weather is bad, or they're really young or old, we'll wait until morning. If they're not down by 9 or 10 A.M., we'll send someone up." The campers are shocked by this. But if we went after every hiker who was unprepared, unfit, or otherwise unready, the staff would die of exhaustion and the park would go bankrupt from all the overtime. This is standard stuff. It says on all our trailhead postings that the responsibility to get back to the car lies with the individual.

Most people are smart enough to pick out a rock, sit and rest their weary glutes, wait until the sun comes up, and pick their way down in the A.M., having learned a sore lesson. Not all, but most.

Bruce really didn't want us to go after this hiker, and he's one of the supervisors most keen to get people down. I was a lot more concerned. The weather was downright nasty, and this hiker was a NOBO—few people know more about hiking than that smelly bunch.

Because he tripped his transponder, I figured he must be in real trouble.

———

"Time to call it."

The radio is hard to hear over the wind. I turn my back to listen.

"Come on down. We don't want you guys up there anymore in this stuff." Bruce sounds tired, too.

In situations like this one—a hasty search in the wee hours after a long day, in worsening weather—we begin to think about diminishing returns. Rescuers tire, which makes them more susceptible to slips, trips, and falls, and the likelihood that they're going to find their subject decreases with every hour. The weather isn't helping, and Justine and I have been stumbling already on the wet ground. Both of us worked an entire shift before setting out on this adventure.

Turning around is the last thing we want to do, though. I hate the idea of leaving anyone up here in this weather. If the guy is injured, he could die from exposure. I feel a deep need to keep looking. I don't even want to consider aborting the search.

While a warm bed sounds good, we both feel we're the best hope this kid has. I consider pretending I can't copy—hearing the radio is difficult when you're in the middle of a gale—but think better of it. Bruce has an unbeatable track record on these things. It is also quite possible, even likely, that our subject is behind us somewhere and we missed him on the way up.

Justine has an idea. "What if he started down the Abol Trail?" she asks. I nod, thinking this might buy us some time. I press the mic on my handheld.

"Let us at least check over to the head of the Abol Trail," I say to Bruce. "There's a chance he might have tried to descend that way."

"All right, but then you're coming down. Let me know when you turn around."

It isn't far to the Abol Trail from Thoreau Spring, and I follow the stone path over to the edge of the Tableland, slipping on the wet rocks and going as close to the mountain's ramparts as I dare. I feel bad crossing the little string fences that mark the way, knowing there is sensitive vegetation all over the place up here. There's a reason only arctic flora grows on this vast plateau, I think to myself, trying to keep upright in the ferocious wind. The climate atop Katahdin is too brutal to allow anything less hardy to take root.

Because I can barely see the ground in front of my headlamp, I'm leery of stepping too far over the lip where the Abol Slide, a long slope of glacially arranged boulders, emerges onto the Tableland. We've had people fall here on nice days. In weather like this, going too far is a ticket to the abyss. If I step in the wrong spot, I could make it down the mountain a whole lot faster than I want.

Still no sign. I feel an emptiness in my gut as I make my way back to Justine, who has been scanning the other side of the trail. Nothing.

At 1:30 A.M., I radio Bruce.

"613 to 54."

"Go ahead."

"We're heading back to the Gateway—but we're going to continue looking on our way down."

With heavy legs and even heavier hearts, we begin our slow descent, intent on dragging out the search as long as we can.

CHAPTER 1

Me, one spectacular July morning: "Great day to be a park ranger, huh, Bob?"
Longtime ranger Bob Howes: "Isn't every day a great day to be a park ranger, Andy?"

I LEFT THESE WOODS JUST SIX MONTHS AGO. I LIVE ON A LOON'S schedule—summer in the North Woods, winter on the coast—and it's amazing how much has changed since I went "10-7," out of service, in November 2020. The road, a narrow old logging thoroughfare, is riddled with sinkholes left behind as the snow and ice reluctantly relaxed their grip just a few weeks ago. I see the telltale lines left by snow sleds grounding out in dirt as I bump along in my old Prius, trying to avoid as many craters as I can. My small hybrid is only a little higher off the ground than a skunk, and it's about the worst vehicle one could drive in the North Woods. But it's what I've got. I have to travel three hours to reach my cabin for my three-day shift, and 45 miles per gallon makes that a lot more tolerable. I hold my breath as I scrape along, hoping I'm not going to poke a hole in my oil pan.

Storms ravaged the roadside since my last drive through the south end of the park. I was up in one of these squalls the month before I left, climbing Katahdin in early October with Ranger Justine Rumaker, looking for a lost AT hiker, and it seems they continued to pound the park afterward. Branches hang just above my roof and jut into both sides of this old tote road. In many places trunks pile on each other in tangles, like the old game of pick-up sticks. Widow-makers, snags, leaners, and springpoles line the road to greet me, green needles stretching out as if to shake hands.

Baxter State Park maintains the road in an unimproved state, in keeping with its "forever wild" mandate. Running all the way up through this great wildlife sanctuary, the 45-mile-long road is dirt and barely two trucks wide, meaning that cars often have to swerve into pullouts or back up when they meet oncoming vehicles. We place limits on the size of vehicles—RVs would scrape their roofs and simply take up too much road. We don't allow motorcycles, either, for motorcyclists' own safety, because people still manage to double the 20-MPH speed limit, cornering like Formula 1 racers. I've seen jeeps swing around bends on two wheels. I've also seen a lot of vehicles several feet off the road in the prickers and huckleberries. Or on their sides. A few on their roofs.

I think back to the end of last season, when I drove some of these roads at high speed myself. I had attended a debrief at the visitor center for a rescue. When we were leaving our meeting, we heard a frantic call for help from Ranger Robin Stevens at Kidney Pond. She had a family in the water . . . in late October. A convoy of trucks flew up this road then, red lights strobing.

Today, it's just me.

When former governor Percival P. Baxter gifted these wildlands to the people of Maine in the early 1930s, he stipulated that the park that bears his name remain a nature preserve and a respite from modern life. We maintain the road in that spirit—it's meant to encourage incoming drivers to go slow, relax, take in the sights. I'm trying to do so today, but I keep fretting about my car's undercarriage. The road isn't usually *this* primitive, I think as I swerve to miss a spruce pointing at my grille like a knight's lance. Nor is it usually this dry. Brown clouds billow 30 feet behind me, like the dust kicked up by a stampede in the desert West, overtaking the car anytime I slow or stop.

I inch along, excited to be back for the start of another season. My off-season, spent at home writing at my computer, gets tedious by January or February. I put on my "freelance fifteen," as I like to call it, and am too plugged in to the digital hive mind for my own comfort. I begin to think about soaring walls of gray granite, reaching up to the blue. Hillsides turning lime green with spring growth. Bear cubs rolling down the bank into the road like something out of Mutual of Omaha's *Wild Kingdom*. Daicey Pond shaking and breaking off the winter weight on its surface, starting to ripple again in spring breezes. Katahdin emerging from beneath the snow and ice, looking more magisterial than ever.

I get antsy.

Sometimes I call up a ranger buddy and pay the park a winter visit, if my schedule allows. On these excursions, I've helped my friend, Bruce White, cut firewood, break trail, transport materials. We were stationed together during my first seasons at the park, and eighteen years later he's my supervisor. Didn't think he liked me much when I started, but we've become good friends since.

Baxter is never wilder than it is under snow cover, never more dangerous or remote, and I'm always keen to venture north for an off-season exploration. A few years back, park officials asked if I wanted to take the seasonal winter ranger job at Chimney Pond. And, boy, did I. But life away from my family is hard enough working one season, never mind two. I didn't even dare broach it with my wife, who struggles with my annual disappearance.

Winters are magic in Baxter Park. I've seen a family of lynx hunting, climbed the mountain, enjoyed the deep quiet of an empty Russell Pond Campground in March, and visited with campers I knew from the summer, who were ensconced in the warm glow of the bunkhouse at South Branch Pond.

But I usually can't get away and instead load weights into my pack and start hiking up Appleton Ridge in my backyard, getting my legs used to trekking uphill carrying 40 pounds. Mine's a sedentary life in the winter, and I quietly become anxious to get back to my duty station in the southwest corner of this big rectangular fastness, savoring the wildness.

Often, the vagaries of climate change prolong my wait. Some years, snow doesn't let go of the road until the end of May, and staff simply can't get in. We'll do projects at headquarters or at the south end, roofing buildings, clearing blowdowns, raking the roadsides, cutting firewood. One year, Bruce and I hiked in 4 miles from the bottom of Abol Hill to Katahdin Stream, becoming de facto backcountry rangers. I helped him open his old duty station, and he helped me begin the process of clearing deadfall at Daicey.

In recent years, we've begun scheduling training sessions for this uncertain time. We'll meet for a week at headquarters with the gang from Wilderness Medical Associates to refresh our Wilderness First Responder credentials, work with the Maine Forest Service (MFS) on Wildland Firefighter certification, or renew our chain saw skills, all to prepare for the upcoming season.

––––––––––

As I creep along the tote road, I can't help but notice the dust coating everything. It's been an unusually dry spring for northern Maine, with rainfall several inches below normal, according to the National Weather Service. *What is normal in 2020?* I think, driving deeper into the state's largest wilderness. One of the things we always hear from returning campers is how excited they are to find the place unchanged, but all I see every year is more change.

In my eighteen seasons as a ranger in these woods, I've watched the climate go through post-traumatic stress disorder. I've seen the moose all but vanish, dropped in their tracks by tens of thousands of winter ticks, which surfed the warmer temperatures north. I've hunkered through ever more violent storms, each one trying to fell more trees than the last. It seems every year for the past several we've witnessed dramatic weather events. We've been drenched by rainstorms that pour down 4 or more inches in 24 hours, almost a third of what Arizona gets in a year. We've been hammered by vicious lightning, lighting up the sky like artillery fire. We've been thrashed by successive October nor'easters, leaving piles of downed trees almost as tall as the young trees left standing. And now drought.

There is no normal anymore.

The head of the Maine Forest Service, Patty Cormier, one of the three members of the Baxter State Park Authority, the board that governs the park, told us during an online May training session that in the first few weeks of spring, her crews had already battled more than 420 blazes across the state—triple the 140 wildfires they had fought the entire previous year. I said to one of my fellow rangers that morning that we would have a fire this season. Within hours, a bunch of year-round rangers excused themselves from our online meeting to go battle a blaze along the Penobscot River in the park's southwest corner. As a former volunteer firefighter, I all but begged Bruce to put me in play but was told I was simply too far away to be of any use. I had to watch on the news like everyone else as Forest Service helicopters dropped water on the flames.

The blaze flashed across the forest floor, finding ready fuel in acres of dead snags and brittle underbrush. We don't cull any of this tinder, as they do in many other places, and I was fearful that this was going to be a big one. Tearing through the West Branch Lands, the fire seemed likely to climb the hill by the Blueberry Ledges and the Appalachian Trail and to sear its way into the park proper, burning up to Katahdin Stream and Abol Campgrounds. Perhaps even all the way to my duty station.

At the end of that day, I finished my Psychological First Aid training session and waited hopefully for a call to head for Millinocket, but it never came. A ranger friend sent me pictures of the Forest Service's Bell helicopter dipping its bucket into the Penobscot and flying back toward the smoke on the hillside, which only made me wish all the more that I had on a fire-resistant Nomex shirt and was blasting water myself.

I've fought one blaze in this part of the park, but it was a minor one. In 2009, Bruce and I were sent down the AT with backpack pumps to extinguish a campfire left by thru-hikers illegally camping alongside the stream. At 8:30 P.M., we made our way down the trail, headlamps illuminating the narrow corridor, scrambling across the big dead snag that hikers had made into a bridge over Nesowadnehunk Stream, until we found the site—marked with a Gatorade bottle atop a stick driven into the ground. The smoldering embers were in a little depression probably 4 feet across.

Bruce took a bunch of pictures for law enforcement, and then we upended our backpack pumps and used them as buckets, dumping 5 gallons at a time onto the fire. We walked a few hundred yards to the river, refilled, and repeated the process over and over. With Pulaski tools—ax on one side, hoe on the other—we broke the surface of the blackened ground and looked for cinders underneath. There were plenty, and we set about dousing. The whole procedure took a few hours, and we arrived back at Daicey Pond exhausted, wet, and sore from backpack pumps banging our shoulder blades. (I suggested to the old chief that we should buy collapsible canvas buckets for such situations, or at least the more modern polymer backpack pumps that form to your back rather than beat on it. He allowed as how these were great ideas but never did anything about it.)

As I went to bed during the latest wildfire, I thought for sure the Blueberry Ledges fire would burn through the night, exhausting our small year-round staff, and the park would need to call in those of us seasonals with firefighting training. I slept lightly and eagerly turned to my phone for messages upon waking. Nothing. Thanks to the Forest Service prioritizing this blaze over several other larger ones nearby—not necessarily because it was Baxter State Park but because it was still small—and diverting air support to it, the conflagration was controlled by morning, burning only 45 acres. The fact that the ground still had moisture in it, below the dry surface, also helped contain the damage.

I learned later that one of my old duty station partners was advocating for me on the fire line—"he'd be great, he used to be a firefighter"—while the gruff park mechanic was cursing me. He said our fire pump was left with water in it over the winter, although I'm pretty sure I put antifreeze in it before I left for the year.

As I climb Abol Hill, I marvel at the desiccated roadsides and think I may end up with a fire to battle yet. At the top of the steep mile-long incline, I wonder what's ahead between Abol and Katahdin Stream Campgrounds. I know from past experience that there is a depression where ice builds up in a long slab, but I've seen very little snow or ice thus far, so I'm not too worried. Back in the day, I wouldn't have even considered taking my Prius across this ice field, but the ground has been so dry I figure it'll be fine.

And it is. A cone on the side of the road shows where one of the year-rounders flagged a hole during an earlier run through the west side of the park. Baxter employs about 60 people total, and only about a dozen year-round rangers (if you count the maintenance guys and foresters among the rangers). This time of year, all of us seasonals return, much to the chagrin of Frank, the burly mechanic who has to ready all our trucks. Ten duty stations are in the park, most of them home to two rangers who split the week in half. Schedules in the backcountry differ, due to the hiking involved in getting to work sites.

My partner, Charity, a native of nearby Millinocket, has already been in to our duty station, texting me a few questions about housing. We've worked together for more than a decade, and I'm hoping there's no truth to the rumors that this is her last season. Her husband, Dean—"L. L. Dean" to some—is retiring from the park after more than fifteen years as a ranger, and word on the street, or the trail, is that she will probably be joining him in a year's time. Charity is in her early 60s, though with her long dark hair she looks closer to her daughter's age, and she's small of stature—"fun size," she likes to say—but big in spirit. She doesn't take any guff from anyone. She'll have to retire sometime, but I'm not looking forward to it. Unlike some partners, we get along great (excepting the fact that she thinks I shouldn't be here at all, having suffered the indignity of coming into the world in a hospital in Norwood, Massachusetts), and I know that when I return from my days off, everything will be in order and she will have gotten a lot of work done. I'm pretty sure she feels the same about me. She's the organized one. I like to joke with the campers that we are good cop and bad cop—they get to decide who's who.

I pilot my Prius under a pair of widow-makers, trees barely suspended above the road, just ready to drop and brain someone, and I'm surprised nobody has felled them yet. As I drive past Katahdin Stream Campground, I notice the eponymous watercourse running beneath the giant new culverts we put in last year, and it's a shadow of its former spring self. The water here usually rages, filled with runoff from on high, but today it's simply babbling.

Soon I'm at Barren Brook, and despite the lack of rain, the black, grass-filled puddle is up near the road. Obviously, Mr. Beaver has been hard at work. These busy, brown, bucktoothed rodents trouble a few locations on the park road on an annual basis, and this half-acre waterway just south of the turnoff to Daicey Pond is one of them. I slow down and scan the surface to see if I can spot any whiskers, but he must be sleeping one off somewhere. The water doesn't look ready to rise over the bank yet, but we'll need to do something about this culvert before the season gets too far along.

I feel my heart thump a bit when I come around the corner and see the Daicey Pond sign. I've been stationed alongside this 35-acre pond for sixteen of my eighteen seasons, and a piece of me never leaves the place. It's become a home.

The signpost seems to list a bit toward the north, and I make a note to straighten it out. I turn down the road toward camp, eager to get an up-close look at the mountain, curious what winter has wrought around the pond, ready for whatever the season brings.

————

My camp is a log cabin in a 3-acre field. A narrow strip of conifers screens it from Daicey Pond Road on one side and wide Nesowadnehunk Stream on the other. On the far side of the field, perhaps 100 yards away, the Appalachian Trail emerges from the woods, crosses Daicey's fourteen-vehicle day-use parking lot, and then reenters the forest on its way to Katahdin Stream and the base of the mountain. Before my time, thru-hikers used to overnight in lean-tos at the side of the meadow, munching on its wild blueberries and raspberries. I am very glad this is no longer the case.

Big and Little Niagara, a series of granite twists and chutes and cascades about a mile away, shush constantly if you listen closely. At night, stars stare down so intently it's astonishing. My driveway ends with a spectacular view of Doubletop, a 3,500-footer with a profile that looks like a child's rendering of a volcano, framed by woods and underscored by the winding Nesowadnehunk Stream. If I were a landscape painter....

I helped build this cabin during my third season stationed at Daicey Pond. The previous year, we raised one much like it in the campground, a rental facility that sleeps six. Built from a kit from a Maine log-home company, my camp has the Lincoln Log aesthetic, and it went together almost as easily. We literally stacked one beveled beam atop the next, applied caulking and a gasket between each one, and spiked them together, usually with a 5-pound hammer while straddling the wall.

I swerve around a few downed trees and pull into my driveway. The camp looks completely different from the outside than it did when I closed the door for the last time in the fall. Back then, it had a porch. That's all been walled in, creating a flat, multicolor front with two different degrees of stain. A small outbuilding for storing tools and firewood stands nearby. That wasn't there last year, either. The steps that once led onto the porch now lead up to Charity's door. Mine is around the corner. Over the winter, the park carpenter and maintenance mechanic, a couple of volunteers, and my supervisor Bruce made my camp into a duplex.

I couldn't be happier.

Daicey is one of the few duty stations in the park where two rangers have to share living quarters. Even when I was at Katahdin Stream in my first season, as a lowly campground attendant probie, I had my own place. Not here. At first, I shared with my previous Daicey partner, Matt, which was fine because our shifts didn't overlap. We were very rarely in the building at the same time.

When Matt moved into maintenance and Charity arrived, she took up residence in the ranger housing at Kidney because her husband, Dean, worked there. That left me with an almost-new three-bedroom with cathedral ceilings. I had the place all to myself. Or so I thought.

The park administrators were soon onto me, however, and decided they could take one of the other rooms to house a trail crew leader. So in came Neil. Then Tony, whose girlfriend, "the Bone Lady," used her trail name exclusively. It was fun to introduce my 10-year-old and his little pal to her—"Guys, this is the Bone Lady"—and watch their eyes grow wide.

Tony and the Bone Lady were great except that they thought long-distance hikers were somehow the Chosen Ones and all others were inferior. A modern hobo, the Bone Lady dumpster-dove her way across the country to visit, but only a few times.

After those two characters came Alan, the English engineer. And then Jon, a retired navy vet who was significantly older than the usual 20-something trail crew boss.

I had no issues with any of them—in fact, I genuinely liked them all. But I have a family, and I'm too old to have a roommate. And the problem with trail crew leaders was that they were off on the weekend when I was working, which meant they were always around. Sometimes they'd spike on a big project somewhere in the park and camp on-site, which was great, and occasionally they'd travel, exploring the state; but more often than not, I'd be trying to write on my lunch break while they chatted with me.

All that's in the past now, I think as I carry boxes to the door, propping it open with my knee. My new camp is much more compact: one bedroom, tiny bath, kitchen and mini living area, with a shared upstairs. But it's all mine. Dean used to call this camp the "Taj," because it was so much nicer than most park housing. He's already renamed it the "Taj Ma Small."

The place is an absolute disaster, filled with construction debris. The remodeling is largely finished, with all the new walls up, their golden pine boards matching the warm wood tone of the interior. It can't be much more than 10 feet from wall to wall, and the big Flame woodstove dominates the space. The kitchen cabinets were torn out of the old visitor center and don't provide enough storage for all my dishes and pans. I'll have to do some fixes here and there to make it right, but the guys did a spectacular job.

And then I notice someone left a turd in my frying pan. On closer inspection, I see that it's a plastic pile of joke-shop poo that one of my winter guests thought was funny. I smile and immediately begin to think of ways to deploy it.

Pan-fried scat and all, I'm very glad to be back.

CHAPTER 2

THE CAMPGROUND IS A MESS. THE SAME STORMS THAT SENT TREES flying into the road pummeled this old sporting camp astride Daicey Pond. As I walk up the steep hill that leads into the parking area, I see small spruces and firs down everywhere: jutting into paths, resting atop outhouses, lying on the ground in sites. The aroma of the pine needles and the minerally smell of the pond are magic, and I breathe deep.

The area around the woodshed looks like an angry Pamola—the spirit the Penobscot natives believed lived atop Katahdin—descended from his perch and walked through, thrashing things with his moose rack and eagle talons. Several spruces are canted over near Cabin 8, including a 60-foot leaner hanging menacingly above the firepit. A big birch crashed to the ground behind the one-room structure, barely missing the roof.

The year-round rangers have already started cutting and cleaning up the debris, creating a massive pile of brush and small trunks that's well over my head, as tall as a cabin and probably longer—which will require at least a dozen trips with the park's 1-ton dump truck. I add this to my extensive list of things necessary to get the campground ready. It will be some job just to pick up all the sticks scattered across the lawn and the parking lot.

Thanks to climate change, every season now seems to begin and end with the clearing of blowdowns. It wasn't that way when I started at the park in the early 2000s. Some areas in the campground enjoy much better views of the mountain than they did just a few years ago.

I walk from cabin to cabin surveying the damage. My duty station is a campground of ten rental camps. Built in the first few decades of the previous century, these log cabins sit all along 36-acre Daicey Pond, five on either side of the ranger station, the parking lot, and a library filled with musty tomes. This old getaway was called Twin Pine Camps, thanks to a pair of sequoia-like eastern white pines smack in the middle of things, and it welcomed hunters and anglers and nature lovers of all kinds for the first half of the twentieth century. The two pines remain today, framing one of the best views of Katahdin to be found, but they continue to drop branches, along with banana-size cones, and I worry they won't be around too much longer. Our cackling neighborhood pileated woodpecker has been plunging their depths for bugs, opening up big cavities. The tops of the trees, once so strong, now look elderly and frail, with sick needles and decaying limbs. You won't notice these infirmities unless you look up, though, because the boles are still straight and stout.

I pause and step onto the dock, which tilts slightly to one side. It's been failing for about a year. The spruce stringers under the cedar decking are rotting, sending screws popping out here and there. Charity and I have been putting in longer screws and toenailing one board to the next, but it's beyond saving. Replacing this 20-foot pier is another project on the docket for the season. Underneath it, the breeze pushes a constant flow of tiny breakers against the shore.

Katahdin is majestic across the pond, with snow still high up on the slopes and in Witherle Ravine, the deep cut between the Hunt Spur and the Owl, a rocky promontory that forms its own peak on the mountain's west side. Staring at the summit from this distance, a 2.5-mile walk from the trailhead, it's very clear why the natives called it "Greatest Mountain." The shore of Daicey enjoys arguably the finest prospect of Katahdin from the west, with the Owl and the long wall of Barren Mountain off to its left and green climbing the slopes everywhere in between. It also offers a great look at the Hunt Spur, the big talus field I was on last October, searching for a thru-hiker who triggered his personal locator beacon. Off to the right is the Abol Slide, another slope of boulders and ledges and one of the oldest routes up the mountain. Hunt and Abol are the two principal thoroughfares on the west side, and I know I'll be heading up them at some point in the season. I always do.

In the coming months, legions of people from all over the world will pose for photographs right here, smiling with the mountain lofting up over their shoulders. I remind myself, as I often do, how lucky I am to have this view at the end of my commute.

Too much to do to pause long today, however. The first week of the season is all about getting the cabins ready for campers. This typically entails pulling the log chairs and cook tables back out onto the porches, hauling the picnic tables into place near the firepits, and taking down the poles we put up from floor to ceiling to help sturdy the camps against the weight of the snow that sits atop them all winter. Four feet of the white stuff puts a lot of stress on half-inch boards and the 6-inch purlins beneath them.

Then it's cleaning, cleaning, cleaning.

The five cabins open for winter camping require special attention. I poke my head into Cabin 5, set directly on the water below the ranger station. With a long porch, room for four, and a panorama out front, it's popular among the regulars. The low-slung structure seems to have weathered the winter well, except that the cold-weather campers were too lazy to use the ash buckets we provided for them, instead dumping their ashes on the ground out front.

When I started at Daicey, I assumed winter visitors would be among the most conscientious folks in the park. These were the hardcore, the old heads, the ones who love the place so much they brave temperatures in the negative teens to be here. And the vast majority of them fit this description. Most come back in the summer, too, and I've gotten to know many. Others, however, seem to feel they can do whatever they want when no ranger is around to check on them. They tuck trash here and there and wear microspikes on the porches and in the buildings, making tiny holes in the floor that fill with dirt and never come clean. They pull off boards and snap the hasps on the woodshed to get at firewood they assume is drier than the stuff in the bays we leave open for them. Some don't even bother to walk to the outhouse.

Charity and I will have to remove the plastic we put over the windows of the winter cabins and pull down the blanket of skirts we nail 4 feet from the base to prevent the wind from blowing up under the camps. (We use an old, thick, felted fabric called mill paper that we acquired from the paper mill in town when it closed, and it seems to do a good job.)

Most years, we paint as many floors and porches as possible and do whatever repairs are vital—we never get to everything that needs fixing on a century-old camp. We've reroofed and repainted all of these buildings since I began at Daicey sixteen years ago. Charity and I have also built countless sets of stairs, replaced railings, and repaired or reconstructed most of the decks. This season Bruce wants to switch out a couple of outhouse risers, which requires new cement floors over the vaults, and to put clear plastic roofing on all of these restrooms, brightening the interiors. We also need to remove and rebuild a ramp that has begun to rot on our accessible cabin. I have a lot of work to do down at my own camp, hauling construction debris up to the burn pile, installing shelving, leveling the new woodshed. Those are just the major projects.

Other than that, it's a lot of brush clearing and raking, getting the lawns by the ranger station, library, and woodshed looking nice. We mow and manicure the grass and rake the paths around the campground so campers don't trip on roots. The tines scraping the grass always make me think about the concept of wilderness.

Are raked lawns wild?

The notion of what exactly constitutes "wild" land recurs periodically at Baxter, where preservation is our primary mission. We get all rhetorical and semantic about terms such as *backcountry* and *frontcountry* and debate how wild the frontcountry is supposed to be. We hash out wilderness zones and what Governor Baxter meant when he said he wanted these woods to be "wild, storm-swept, untouched by man," a "place where nature rules and where the creatures of the forest hold undisputed dominion." The park administration has to interpret the governor's words, trying to maintain this place as he wanted, which is no easy task in a world where the tentacles of technology seem to penetrate everywhere.

I think of all the blackflies I've killed. Technically, each one is a creature of this forest. The concept of wilderness is tricky, debated far and wide. Baxter himself called for a "rough, but passable motor road," and "small cabins for mountain climbers" in his park, which sounds a lot like what we have at Daicey Pond. He also specified that he didn't have much use for "modern civilization with its trailers and gasoline fumes, its unsightly billboards, its radio and jazz" encroaching on the Maine wilderness. At least not *his* wilderness.

I'm not real big on the radio or jazz, either.

The governor proclaimed that "the sound of the axe and of falling trees never will echo through these forests." I wonder what he would think of the sound of a chain saw, cutting through hazard trees?

———————

I haul out my trusty orange Husqvarna chain saw and poke around the garage for our chaps and helmet. The year-round rangers like to borrow our tools in the off-season, and we often return to empty gas cans and dull saws. I pull the scabbard off, and sure enough, the chain is full of chips. I put the bar into the vise on our workbench, giving the teeth a thorough going-over with a file. I'm not much good at sharpening, but I've found a method that works for me and can get my chain in the ballpark.

When I'm finished, I snap on my chaps and haul all my gear up to Cabin 8 to fell the scary widow-maker, glad no one else is around. I prefer to saw on my own, in case I mess things up. I'm an adequate sawyer and can accomplish what I need to, but I don't always do it in the most orthodox manner. I haven't dropped a tree on a building yet, despite some that were listing within a few feet of a cabin, and I still have all my parts. But I'm no expert, so I'm glad we have a first aid kit stuffed with wound dressings on the belt of our chaps.

Last season began with another menacing spruce, about 18 inches in diameter, that snapped 5 feet off the ground and hung above the path to Cabin 3. It was twisted and broken enough that I could put my hand through it, held together by 6 or 7 inches of fiber, which stretched up for 15 feet, under enormous stress. The tree was only a yard from Cabin 5, and if I cut it wrong, the butt would have crashed right through the south wall. Or exploded all over me, thanks to the pent-up force. Charity and I managed to get it down with the help of a rope and a come-along winch—everything, including me, under a massive amount of tension. I made a bunch of small cuts to release the energy slowly and cranked on the winch until the tree was down. It didn't help my blood pressure.

This particular leaner isn't that bad, but it's still one to get the nerves going, a tall spruce blown from Cabin 8's site toward Cabin 7, where it got snagged in a bunch of similar-size trees. It's canted at about a 60-degree angle, and my plan is to saw it in several stages, making successive Y notches, cutting sections until the tree drops enough to untangle from the branches above. The angry screech of the saw echoes off the mountain. The rangers at Kidney Pond can probably hear it if they are around.

Well, the idea was a good one, but it doesn't work as planned. The base of the leaner falls, which I wanted it to do, but every time it does, it shifts closer to the standing trees, until eventually the trunk is almost upright. It gets to the point where if I cut it any more, I won't have time to get out from underneath when it lets go above.

I do some swearing and pacing, glad the park is still closed to the public and I'm the only ranger for a few miles.

Bruce has a mantra he tells probies: Always use the truck. If you're faced with a problem and you can drive to it, you have a very powerful tool at your disposal. That seems to be the obvious play here. Cabin 8 is one of the few camps at Daicey Pond accessible by vehicle. I can back up the truck, tie a rope to the base of the tree, and drag it until it's at a safe enough angle to cut.

Again, right idea, but it doesn't pay off. The slope of the ground is such that the base of the tree digs in and hardly moves. I thought the brute force of the truck would be able to dislodge it but no go.

I walk in circles and curse some more. The tree is an even bigger hazard now.

I trot back to the shop—Charity and I get a lot of exercise between the cabins and the garage, always needing some tool—and grab the come-along and some rope. Now I can change the direction I haul the base, so I can pull it away from the other trees and downhill rather than into the hill.

This works.

The job takes many more hours than I wanted it to, a lot of sweat, some foul language, and a few nervous moments, but I get the tree down and buck it up, throwing the pieces onto the debris pile.

Now it's off to Cabin 3 . . . where there's a tree that's even worse.

CHAPTER 3

"Daicey Pond is 10-8," I say, sliding into the chair in the ranger station. The clock on the old government-gray desk reads 6:46 A.M.

"Kidney Pond is 10-8," the radio barks back at me.

"10-4 Daicey, 10-4 Kidney," responds Togue Gate. Sounds like Cindy, a new gatekeeper whose voice I recognize from radio traffic, although I've only met her a couple of times.

The park has been open for barely a week, and we've already had nine search-and-rescue (SAR) events. The most dramatic was the airlift of a 31-year-old woman off the Knife Edge, capably handled by Chimney Pond ranger Jen Sinsabaugh and resource director Mike Pounch, which delighted TV news stations and gave the park's director an opportunity to remind folks that the "Mountain of the People of Maine" is not an easy outing.

"A lot of people are underestimating Mount Katahdin," Eben Sypitkowski told the local news. "If you're on the couch now, going from the couch to Katahdin is not a very good way to go."

Hard to argue that.

Today, at least, doesn't sound too busy. You can usually tell how frantic things are at the gate by how quickly gatekeepers answer you on the radio. Some Saturdays they're looking at a traffic jam of which Los Angeles could be proud, and they have no time or inclination to talk.

Morning often starts slowly at Daicey, which is one of the reasons I jumped at the chance to transfer here when a position opened after two seasons at Katahdin Stream Campground. Much as I loved being a mountain ranger, those seasons were nonstop. Here the situation is much more placid. I can stand on the dock and watch the sunrise burn its way across the top of the mountain.

Katahdin never looks the same—the clouds and light, the colors of the seasons, all write themselves across its bulk—and I enjoy its many moods. I like listening as the birds start to twitter in the trees. Sometimes I see early anglers whipping their fly rods back and forth across the pond, as if they're trying to hypnotize the trout. Campers straggle out from their cabins in their pajama bottoms, walk to their vehicles to pick up a forgotten item, check the weather on the kiosk by the library, or step to the outhouse for their morning constitutional. We all ease into the day.

My Katahdin Stream partner Bruce White called me "cabin boy" when I put in for this duty station. He'd been at the base of the mountain for decades. Little did he know he'd be leaving Katahdin Stream in a few years, too, taking a job as part of the year-round staff "infection," as he used to call the park's nonseasonals. He finally got the position he had always wanted and long deserved, and he eventually took oversight of Daicey and Kidney and Katahdin Stream and Abol on the same schedule as mine, essentially running the day-to-day of the park's west side. Once comparable to a staff sergeant in the field, the guy who had the respect of all the grunts and made the decisions that matter where they mattered, Bruce became the equivalent of an officer. He took the unit number 54 and joined the ranks of the "Fives," the year-round supervisory rangers. Although now the burly, balding ranger had to learn to tuck in his shirt, wear his badge, and spend more time in meetings at headquarters.

I saw the move to this old sporting camp as a real opportunity for my family. First, it was a promotion and a raise, going from campground attendant to actual ranger. Second, it was better housing. I told my wife it was like having a summer home paid for by the state of Maine. She and our 2-year-old, Gus, could stay with me in the big cabin, and they could paddle and swim and hike away their Julys and Augusts. Of course, I'd be working, but this job was generally calmer than Katahdin Stream, and I'd be more likely to be available and around. So the thinking went.

I am around for the most part, but rangers, I found, are always busy. Daicey sees a rotating cast of characters that is fairly constant—anglers come in May and June to enjoy one of the finest fisheries in the Northeast, famous for its native trout; families follow when school lets out; foliage seekers visit in autumn, when anglers return—and it keeps us running. Many campers are regulars, and I've watched their kids grow, enlisting hundreds into the ranks of the junior rangers.

Getting to know these folks is one of the perks of the job. They come from all over, and Charity and I can predict who will be in which cabin when with a scary degree of accuracy. The family groups from Freeport and Brunswick and Harpswell, made up of architects and teachers. The chef from Bowdoinham and his family. The photographer from Portland. The German diplomat from the U.N. The woman from Tokyo, who returns almost every year despite the distance. The multigenerational family from Cumberland. The artist from central Massachusetts. The couple and their artistic son from Stonington. The steeplejack and gardener from Edgecomb. The women from Maine Med. Longtimers from L.L.Bean. The writers from Blue Hill. The Lewiston teacher. And the Civil War–reenacting volunteer who has taught me a lot about carpentry. I'm honored to be a part of the backdrop of their annual vacations. And I feel just as privileged to watch newcomers become enchanted with Baxter Park, to see their cares and concerns lift away with each successive day spent beside the pond.

The cabins they rent are simple: just bunks, a woodstove, and a gas light. No running water. No bedding. I tell people that these camps are essentially like tents—you bring everything you would if you were tenting—except that they keep you up off the ground and put a roof over your head. Outside each one you'll find a fire ring and a picnic table and a path to the outhouse. We provide hardwood to keep visitors warm in the shoulder seasons and little handcarts to transport gear from the parking lot.

Each of these small dwellings has a character—"parkitecture"—all its own. Cabin 1 features floor-to-ceiling wraparound windows and a nice little waterfront. Cabin 2 was built from the marriage of two other camps and consequently sags a lot in the middle (not a cabin for playing marbles). Cabin 4, too, was made from conjoined camps, and squirrels love the insulation in its roof. Cabins 3 and 7 are single rooms that accommodate only two people. Cabin 9 had massive chains that once kept its long porch from blowing off. Cabin 10 is new construction, which means it is clean and tight but features insulated doors that remind me of a warehouse.

Some are closer to the pond and the outhouses and the woodshed than others. The vast majority have a buffer of trees between them, allowing a modicum of privacy. The woods don't prevent sound from carrying, however, thanks to the amphitheater effect of the pond, and I frequently have to go around at night and ask people to lower the volume. One of my favorite tricks is to repeat big-voiced campers' words back to them, verbatim. "I can't believe you think Bob was really gonna leave Sally," I'll say, and they'll look at me, astonished.

"Sally could probably hear that, too."

———————

Nobody's making any noise this morning, though. My job doesn't always begin so tranquilly at Daicey Pond. Just a few days ago, I was summoned to my first rescue of the season before I was even technically on duty. I had just signed on, hadn't even eaten my breakfast bar, when Bruce radioed and told me to grab my fast pack, the stuffed fanny belt we use to carry our most essential first aid gear. A woman had hurt her lower leg, one of the most common injuries we see, at the base of the Blueberry Ledges on an early morning walk, and I was to meet up with Ranger Jesse Laporte from Abol Campground and hike in with a SAR team.

"Pick up a boot at Katahdin Stream," Bruce reminded me. These big plastic splints often allow us to walk patients with unstable ankles rather than carry them. Anything is better than carrying. I grabbed it and drove for a half hour on old logging roads, out of the south end and around the base of the park, just to reach the trail for the 2-mile trek in. I hadn't been down to this part of the park since the previous October, when I took an on-duty hike with our AT steward, and the Blueberry Ledges area was where the big fire had been in the spring, so I was happy to go and check things out. Although it had only been weeks since the burn, little green shoots were already pushing up through the charred forest floor.

As Jesse and I got close to the scene, we could hear screaming. We hustled along and found a woman in her 40s sitting in the trail in a great deal of pain. She had come down hard on her left leg and something snapped. She wasn't walking anywhere, and we ended up carrying her out on a Stokes with the help of the SAR team. We used a carrying system pioneered by Baxter Park, which consists of interlocking backpacks that allow us to shoulder most of the weight of the litter on our backs rather than solely using our arms. Four rangers or volunteers each wear a pack that is attached by a pole to the rescuer across the stretcher from them. Straps hang down from these braces to the litter, and a team can comfortably carry an injured person for a half-mile or more. The contraption only works on a wide enough walkway, but the conditions on this section of the Appalachian Trail were ideal for the application, and out we went. It took us about an hour to get the injured woman to the ambulance crew from Millinocket, who parked just off the Golden Road. All the travel used up much of my morning.

Most Daicey days ease in more gradually. I can even put my feet up on the desk and chomp a Pop-Tart—brown sugar cinnamon, of course—as I record the weather. Today is one of those Pop-Tart days. Nobody's moving, and the pond is still. Many mornings, campers stop by the office to make a reservation, hit me up for hiking tips, or ask for a canoe key. (We have rental boats on ponds all across the Daicey-Kidney area. Most are short hikes in, and we lock them in place; otherwise some visitors would help themselves—locals will occasionally liberate canoes from their racks by stomping on the thwarts until they break—and people would hike all the way in only to find no canoes available. We've had fistfights start this way.)

While I'm always up for adventure, it's nice if it arrives around midday rather than hitting you in the face at sunrise.

———————

The office is a long, narrow space that used to be the porch of this old building. We have our base radio beside the desk; a couple of guest chairs; a long bench; and a little cabinet Charity built to house emergency gear, display books and maps for sale, and our guest ledger.

The huge old register looks like a spell book from Hogwarts and is filled with the notes and signatures of campers and thru-hikers dating back to the mid-1970s. Once or twice a year, a visitor will pore through its contents to find their name from a trip long ago. We're reaching the last few of its parchment-like pages and will have to make a decision about what to do with the dusty volume. Does it remain at Daicey for future guests to enjoy, or does it go to the archives at HQ?

A map of the park, a map of the AT, a picture of Governor Baxter, a drawing of Pamola, and a bunch of memos and lists occupy the walls. I glance up at the ten-codes pinned beside the desk. They look as bureaucratic as possible, typed on an old Smith Corona, and I think how strange it is to talk in a numerical, encoded language. To my colleagues, I'm now 6-13. Before that I was 77 (informally, Double Oh-77). Way back, at Katahdin Stream, I was Unit 5, and my toddler son, Gus, was jokingly referred to as Unit 0.5 or "Point Five."

My inner 10-year-old, fed a diet of cop shows on TV, loves this stuff. I hope we never make the move to plain language in an effort to simplify communication, as many first responders and the National Park Service have in the aftermath of 9/11. If the ten-codes were to go, I'd miss them. I still get a kick out of grabbing the radio in my truck and saying, "10-3" whenever anyone's looking for me.

Ten-codes were put into operation about the same time the park was founded, both for brevity and to keep things difficult to follow for anyone listening to a police scanner. (Plenty of people in Millinocket have scanners tuned to park radio traffic. I assume they've figured out what our codes mean by now.) The Association of Police Communications intro-duced the idea of ten-codes in a 1935 issue of its *APCO Bulletin*, borrowing the notion from the U.S. Navy's use of Morse code. Agencies everywhere began to use them widely in the '40s and '50s, and each one customized them a little. Probably nothing made ten-codes more widely known than TV and movie first responders talking into their shoulders and the 1975 C. W. McCall crossover hit "Convoy."

Baxter's radio codes parallel those used by the Maine State Police. Like other agencies, we try to keep radio traffic to a minimum, something a lot of probies have a hard time comprehending, and we use a bunch of ten-codes to that end.

Everyone's heard 10-4, which technically means "I acknowledge" but is often substituted for yes. "Are you on your way to the scene?" someone will ask. "10-4."

We use 10-1 for having difficulty copying, or hearing. Some rangers drop this in when they don't like what their supervisor is telling them: "Sorry, you're really 10-1." The gate and HQ often employ it to make rangers slow down or to have them repeat something. It can get loud at those stations and hard to hear. When we're coming in 10-2, or loud and clear, we can continue.

Every morning I sign on for my 7 A.M. shift with: "Daicey Pond is 10-8," which means I'm in service or on duty. It's the reverse in the evening: "Daicey Pond is 10-7," or out of service/away from the radio, though I never really am because I keep the radio with me when I go down to my cabin in case of emergency. This procedure not only indicates where all the rangers are during the day but also shows who's late to work. It can also be a sign that someone has a day off and no one scheduled a replacement. If I don't hear Kidney Pond go 10-8 in the morning, I'll usually drive over and post the weather and clean their toilets.

Sometimes I'll go 10-7 midday when I'm using the chain saw or the lawn mower, and it's too loud to hear radio traffic. Occasionally a ranger who's not yet comfortable with these Texas-massacre machines calls

"10-7 chain saw" repeatedly until someone 10-4s, just so everyone knows they've fired up and might be bleeding soon.

Rangers also go 10-7 when they're leaving their duty stations to hike, and again, this is so someone knows where they are. When I started at the park it was typical for rangers to call themselves off duty for their lunch break, but it doesn't happen that much anymore. I never did so because if something exciting goes down, I'd much rather be doing *that* than whatever afternoon project I have planned.

We only use a handful of ten-codes, but the ones we use, we use a lot. It's really common to hear rangers ask others for their 10-20, or location. Supervisory rangers, who travel to places where cell-phone service is a possibility, will occasionally ask each other for a 10-21, which means phone call. (Many of our rescues begin with a 10-21 to 911.) A 10-42 is a dog in the park, all too common, unfortunately. (Everyone now can print fake papers to claim their Chihuahua is a service animal.) An individual having mental problems is 10-44. A vehicle accident is 10-55.

We have a couple of less usual codes, too. On a serious emergency, when, for example, a helicopter is trying to communicate with rangers on the ground, a supervisor may call a Signal 1000. This is another state police code—"Emergency Radio Silence"—effectively stopping all nonessential communication. It prevents the Roaring Brook ranger from calling HQ to check on the availability of tent site 17 while a Black Hawk is circling, searching for an injured person. We used to call Code K for a fatality to avoid having to transmit words like *death* or *body* or *corpse*.

Legendary north end gatekeeper Dana Miller, who spent a couple of decades welcoming visitors to Matagamon Gate, obviously liked ten-codes, too. He used every one possible when he read the weather in the morning:

"Matagamon Gate to all Baxter State Park stations, please 10-23 for the 10-13, 10-36, 7 A.M." Which meant "please stand by for the weather, the correct time is . . . " And he always sounded like he was smiling when he said it.

CHAPTER 4

THE CALL COMES IN JUST BEFORE I SIGN OFF AT 9 P.M. THE PARK administration like us to hold office hours in the ranger station for an hour in the morning and an hour at night to be available to campers who have questions, want to buy a map, or need keys for canoes on remote ponds. Otherwise, as I tell my campers, we "range by definition." Many nights, no one shows up. That's been the case this evening, and I'm reading under the gas light when Bruce calls and puts me on standby. He tells me there's an injured hiker on the Hunt Trail and to get a pack together and be ready to head up if the situation turns out to be more than a simple dehydration walk-down.

Standby is a kind of purgatory for a ranger—you're not yet going to help, but you have to remain available and attached to the radio. When you're chain sawing or mowing the lawn or working someplace where the signal is poor, this can be problematic. I often feel l can't get much done when I'm standing by, and in some cases you can wait for hours before being told to stand down. Sometimes the duty officer forgets to call, and you're in an even greater state of limbo. Sounds like the situation is resolved but you can't be sure. The worst situation is when you get alerted that you might be needed in the middle of the night. I'm a sound sleeper, so I can't rest because there's a good chance I'll be dead to the world when the call comes in.

Occasionally we even get sent to the trailhead to stand by. A couple of years ago, we passed a whole afternoon waiting to find out whether the

Forest Service was going to be able to pluck a patient off the Abol Trail. There was a chance many of us would be needed to carry the injured individual from the current location to a spot higher up the mountain from which they could be reached by air. Five or six of us stood around in the park's Caribou Pit landing zone for three or four hours before we were dismissed back to our duty stations, and it was a bummer because it would have meant a helicopter ride to the summit.

But tonight I'm at my desk and not too worried. This sounds like one of our most frequent customers—a hiker too exhausted to continue, who has sweated or vomited out all liquids, feeling sickly. Simple fatigue ranks second only to lower extremity injuries as the reason for SAR callouts at the park. Combined with dehydration and under-preparedness, it almost rises to the top. Fatigue is considered "causative" in 66 percent of our medical calls.

Typically, these incidents go like this: we hike up and the subject is relieved to see a ranger. We have them sit up, take small sips of watered-down Gatorade, and munch on salty crackers. They tell us they can't keep anything down but manage to take on enough water and electrolytes to feel dramatically better pretty quickly. Usually within an hour we're moving them down the trail. In old rescue parlance this process is known as "feed 'em and beat 'em."

These hikers shuffle slowly, and we steady them with a gentle hand on the arm as they tell us how the mountain was "way harder than they thought." It takes several hours, depending upon how high up we are, but we get them down with little difficulty. In the parking lot, they thank us repeatedly for "saving their lives," and then go to sleep it off. Some go to the ER; most feel so improved and relieved to be back roadside they don't bother.

Our protocol is to let exhausted people rest and then make their own way down whenever possible . . . unless they call for help. In other words, we don't go after them. Many people are surprised by this, but if we mounted a rescue for every party that discovers Katahdin is a real mountain and gets "spaghetti legs" from sheer exhaustion, we'd be up there constantly and too fatigued ourselves to be ready for genuine emergencies. Unless we know of an injury or someone calls 911, we don't go.

I can't count the number of walk-downs I've done over the years, and they almost all follow this same script.

Which is why I'm a little surprised when the duty officer, Russ Closs, radios Bruce from the trail: "We're going to shelter in place for the night and then fly her in the morning." By this time it's 11 P.M. I've gone off duty and am reading but also listening to park traffic, just in case.

After hearing this transmission, I wrap my hand around the strap of my pack before Bruce even calls, knowing full well I'll be acting as Sherpa, hauling supplies up the trail.

Wait for it . . .

"54 to 613."

I reach for my handheld.

"10-3."

Wait . . .

"Grab your pack and head for Katahdin Stream."

Knew it.

"10-4."

Everything I'd heard on the radio—you always follow keenly when something's going on, like a 1930s kid in the parlor listening to a serial on a vacuum-tube console—suggests this is a classic case of dehydration. The temperature during the day was in the high 80s, and the humidity was thick, the kind where perspiration constantly flows down the back of your legs just walking around the campground. It's still muggy and in the 70s several hours after sundown. It sounds to me like this woman simply met her match in Katahdin.

As tonight's duty officer, Russ Closs is responsible for making the big decisions. About 30, with a new son, he arrived this spring from a small park in Pennsylvania, where he served as a law enforcement ranger. When he got the call about a woman in distress on the Hunt Trail, he decided it would be a good idea to check out the trail himself, since it was one of several on the mountain he'd yet to hike. He brought Kevin, a probie stationed at my old duty station, Katahdin Stream, along with him to get more experience in mountain rescue.

Now they need two more.

I chuck my pack onto the passenger seat and drive down to Katahdin Stream, wondering. The ranger station is aglow when I arrive, surrounded by the pervasive blackness of a Baxter night, and it looks like a truck rally, so many ranger vehicles are parked out front. I find a spot for mine and make my way to the office, where Bruce and supervisory ranger Russ Porter are busy gathering supplies by the light of the propane lamp: The shelter we need. Sleeping bags for the patient and her husband. Petzl helicopter helmets. Foam pads. Ubiquitous blue tarps for any number of uses. More food, more water.

"Hey—why are we going up after a dehydration case?" I ask Bruce, drawing it out like a perturbed teenager. Since we're now old friends, I can say pretty much whatever I want to him without risk of getting fired.

He spins around on me, serious.

"You didn't hear about the chest pains and radiating left arm pain?"

I allow as how I missed that. Radio communication is a perennial problem in Baxter Park. The massive granite wall between campgrounds does a very effective job of preventing us from speaking to and hearing one another clearly. The staticky airway often delivers only one side of a conversation, and we have to extrapolate.

When I'm walking around with a handheld in my back pocket, for example, I can't pick up much other than the two neighboring stations, the visitor center, and sometimes the gate. My truck radio brings in the gate, headquarters, and most of the south end, and the base radio in the ranger station does better still, reaching the other side of the mountain and the north end. But the small Motorola two-way that I have on me at all times is very limited. At night, I place it atop the propane refrigerator in my cabin, hoping the metal will serve as an antenna for reasons such as this, when there are emergencies nearby. Bruce is one of two supervisory rangers who overnights in the park—most now live in town—and our shifts overlap. I know he'll call if something's going on.

But I heard nothing of a heart attack.

"Do you want to be the guy who watches her drop from a heart attack at O'Joy Brook as you walk her down?" he asks me.

I allow as how I don't want to be that guy.

So, Porter and I begin our way up the Hunt Trail a little before midnight. Our mission is to hike the supplies up and come straight back down. The campground is full but quiet as we walk briskly toward the trailhead. A couple of tents glow from inside. A party is still at a campfire and they nod as we march past, our plastic helicopter helmets quietly thumping off our packs.

Russ Porter is roughly half my age, newly returned from the Maine Criminal Justice Academy. A local boy from Millinocket—whenever I've been in town with him, he's pointed out a different cousin—he started on the trail crew and worked his way up to a supervisory position. He oversees the north end under our new district ranger and remains one of the good guys, sympathetic to the seasonals because he was one. Officially, he's in the south end tonight providing backup to duty officer Russ Closs. Russ and Russ.

"You don't need to wait for me," I say as we hit the trail proper, paralleling the rushing stream. My knees are sore from the bursitis that has been bothering me all season, and I don't want to hold him back.

"No rush," he says, telling me he's still recovering from a lower leg stress fracture he got at the academy. We make good time anyway, periodically radioing our position to Bruce, who has his feet up on the desk at the Katahdin Stream station, serving as our relay.

Within an hour, we climb up past O'Joy Brook, a tiny seep that burbles across the trail despite the dry summer. We both expect to find our patient in the trail not too far thereafter, but up we keep going. And it is *up*. The Hunt Trail, a.k.a. the Appalachian Trail, takes a much more direct route to the summit after it passes the brook. It's another half hour before we hear voices over our own huffing and puffing.

Then we see lights in the trail a steep climb above us and know we are there. Closs reports our arrival to Bruce back at the station, who adds the information to the notes he's keeping of the event. We drop our gear and introduce ourselves to the patient, who is sitting on a rock next to her husband. She's 53 years old and dark haired, with a nice smile—when she isn't grimacing from pain. The couple are from Massachusetts, and she tells us they've done a lot of hiking, including Mount Washington, "which was way easier than this," but I wonder how true that is.

There's not much we can do for a heart case other than keep her warm, dry, and calm. The official treatment, according to our Wilderness First Responder training, is PROP: position of comfort, rest, O_2, and positive pressure ventilation if she starts to have difficulty breathing. We offer a sleeping pad and a down bag, and she's happy to take them, putting her space blanket on top. Then we string up a little triangle tent over her with our tarp and some paracord to keep her out of the gathering mist. A light rain seems imminent.

"I hope you'll still give us a good review on Yelp," Kevin jokes as we get her settled for the evening. We all crack up, even the patient. I guess this little yuk comes from Kevin's time working in Portland restaurants, and I file it away for later use. A skinny guy with a wispy horseshoe mustache—a self-described "dirty hippie"—Kevin's excited to be on his first helicopter rescue.

"Anyone given her aspirin?" I ask. The little analgesic is, of course, ideal for heart issues.

No one has. Kevin and I look in our respective fast packs. We give her a pill and some water, and she gulps both down. She doesn't seem to me like she is going to die soon, and I am still not convinced she is suffering from anything beyond dehydration, but I keep my counsel. Though I am the most senior ranger on the scene, with years on Russ Porter and certainly Russ Closs and Kevin, I am twice outranked. Thrice if you count Bruce, running the show at the base of the mountain. And I don't want to be the guy who gets her killed.

Porter and I prepare to head back down the trail, but first we all huddle. Closs and Kevin don't want us to leave. It becomes clear that the two newbies could use our help. Porter and I have both been involved with helicopter rescues before. Neither of these guys have.

"We may need to carry her up the trail if she can't walk," Closs says. "That would require more than the three of us." He points at himself, Kevin, and the husband.

Porter and I look at each other and realize they are right. We are stuck here. Then it starts to drizzle.

We report all this to Bruce and then pick spots in the trail and try to rest. We have several hours until daylight and with it the Black Hawk. I find a patch of moss, surrounded by roots and rocks. Everything in Baxter is roots and rocks.

Kevin starts snoring almost instantly, feet in the trail, his head propped up on a helicopter helmet on the bank. He doesn't seem bothered by the mist wrapping this side of Katahdin like a cloud or by the roots and stones underneath him. Other than his heavy breathing, all is quiet way up here on Hunt Trail, but you'd expect that at 2 A.M.

"He got the comfortable rock," Russ Porter quips as he settles into a spot down the trail. "Mine's a little lumpy."

We close our eyes and try to catch some z's, taking turns looking after our patient.

———————

As the sun begins to warm the sky, rising over the mountain's eastward shoulder, we break camp. I check on the woman. She's still feeling sick, but we convince her to have a few bites to eat and a few sips to drink. Then we pack the cold-weather gear into our rucks. Porter and I take down the blue tarp and lay it out on the trail, then roll hiking poles into the sides for handles to improvise a litter. We've done this in training sessions. In our search-and-rescue classes, we make a game of experimenting with different carrying systems, trying all kinds of makeshift stretchers, and I've even employed a couple when it counted.

Bruce and I once piggybacked a small woman down from the Table-land using pretzeled-up 2-inch webbing straps to create a harness/

backpack with slots for her legs, support for her fanny, and a length we could extend over our shoulders to hold on to. We took turns hiking down with her on our backs, whining in our ears—exhausting but effective. Porter and I are pretty sure we can make our litter work, but we hope that our new friend from Massachusetts can walk the steep quarter-mile ahead. Any rescue where a patient can walk is a good rescue, and she'd be a heavy carry uphill with just five of us.

We leave her brilliant orange space blanket, which did a great job keeping her warm all night, on top of the litter as a signal for the helicopter. The bright, reflective fabric is a perfect contrast to the black-green trees and gray granite slabs and should attract the attention of the pilot and the crew, which can be tricky up here surrounded by miles of trees and rocks.

Closs checks in with Bruce, who's been up all night beside the radio at the Katahdin Stream station. I'm sure we caught him dozing a couple of times, but he was always ready for business when we called. Closs tells him we're going to start up the trail and see how far we can get. Bruce says the bird is scrambling a team together.

We get the patient on her feet and take the tentative first steps up the trail. She's shaky but game. We try to make her laugh as much as possible. This is an age-old trick, and it typically works. Get people chuckling, and they'll forget how much pain they're in. If you don't have any good jokes and stories, simply asking patients questions and making conversation can distract from the discomfort.

She stumbles several times on the rocky path, but always with a ranger at her elbow to catch her. Soon, she tells us she needs to use the bathroom. This often happens on rescues. When the patient is prostrate in a Stokes litter, wrapped up like a burrito in a sleeping bag covered in plastic for warmth, this can be a real time-consuming pain in the ass (we always try to make sure they don't have to go before we wrap them, but sometimes it happens anyway). Urine breaks can also be a challenge when patients are in debilitating pain or have broken bones or other conditions that make it difficult to get them to a private spot off-trail, in which case you just have to make do. Sometimes we use makeshift diapers and they do what needs to be done in the litter.

This time is easy, though. We simply find one of the natural openings on the side of the Hunt Trail, probably created by hikers for this very reason, and leave her in the capable hands of her husband. Then we retreat to give her some privacy.

As the trail approaches treeline, it climbs over a few real knee stretchers, which require some negotiation and slow us as we begin again, but we manage, shambling, one small step after another, ever upward toward the gray sky above. I begin to worry that the clouds might impede our flying cavalry.

And then we're there: Rescue Rock, so named because it's one of the best places—really one of the only places—on this section of the trail where a helicopter has a clear expanse from which to hoist.

A massive erratic projecting 20 feet over the trail as it breaks the treeline, this glacial boulder creates a recessed cavity with two pathways around it. We head left, where there are more stunted trees for handholds, and our patient waves for us to stop almost immediately.

She bends at the waist and vomits between her feet, retching several times. She seems in agony, growling and then heaving, until it's clear she has nothing left in her stomach and is just spasming. After a few minutes, she straightens up, wipes her mouth, and apologizes. We do what we can to comfort her.

When she's able to continue, we make the steep climb up the bank beside Rescue Rock, using roots to help pull ourselves and our patient the 20 remaining yards to a resting place just behind the crown of the erratic. We sit her on a natural granite bench and wrap the tarp around her shoulders against the cold. Then the four of us scramble the last 10 feet up onto the rock itself, using finger holds and roots, to figure out next steps. If the litter lands on the 5-by-10 square top of this boulder, which we're expecting, we'll have an awkward time trying to get her up the nearly vertical side.

Above us the gray is giving way to blue as the drizzle from last night blows off to the east, the scene framed by the last stubborn evergreens.

We have a fantastic view out to the west, over the valley carved by Katahdin Stream. From here the woods seem almost endless—we're not high enough yet to see roads or buildings, just the roof of the forest as it trundles across everything.

We unfurl the space blanket on the rock, which juts up like a little island in the sky. Our radios crackle. Bruce reports that the Guard helicopter is "probably a half hour out."

Closs acknowledges this happy intel. Kevin ties strips of orange flagging tape to the ends of his hiking poles to make a moving signal, like the people with the lights on an airport runway. I jump down and talk to the patient and her husband. She's nervous about being winched off the mountain in a basket but too sick to complain much. Her husband stands off to one side. He's been quiet for much of the time and seems even more so now that this airlift thing is becoming a reality. We try to reassure him that everything will be fine, that she's in the best hands with the Guard, who are experts at extraction.

The bird is now about fifteen minutes out, and the chief calls a Signal 1000. All those rangers just coming on duty down below will have to lay off the radio until the patient is onboard the helo—rescue in progress, no unnecessary chatter. This allows the pilot to communicate with us on the ground, unimpeded.

I talk to Closs and Porter, and we agree I should trot down the trail to create a perimeter. We always keep hikers a few hundred yards away when we perform helicopter evacuations so that bystanders don't get whacked by debris or strafed with gravel. Even though it's just 6:30 in the morning, a few sturdy folks are already well along on their way up the Hunt Trail.

The last medevac I worked, another all-nighter with an early morning airlift, I hiked down the Abol Trail and asked a young, fit, 30ish woman dressed in the latest hiking tights to please stop where she was.

"Hang out here," I said. "We have a helicopter arriving momentarily to lift an injured hiker, and we don't want you to get hit by a flying rock." She looked at me with a frown, her eyes rolled up to her brow, and then she groaned, looking at her watch.

"*Really?*" she whined.

I was dumbfounded.

"Really," I said. Her record time was apparently more important than our broken person. She was about to witness one of the most interesting things a hiker can see, a short-haul, human external cargo, off the side of the mountain, but was pissed she had to pause.

We've seen this before. Years ago, a guy tried to kill himself with a hacksaw blade to the Adam's apple, sitting in an open tent in full view of the Abol Trail. All morning, hikers walked past, none bothering to turn around and tell a ranger, which might have delayed their ascent by a half hour at most. My partner Charity, who was stationed at Abol then, didn't hear about this guy bleeding out until the afternoon. Thankfully, despite all the blood, he only did superficial damage, but I was astonished at how myopic climbers can be.

This morning, I find two middle-aged women bounding up the trail. I give them my spiel. "I hope everyone's OK," one of them says. I ask them to keep a cordon, and they seem honored and excited to help. *That's more like it*, I think, trotting back into position.

As I reach the patient, the thrum of the inbound helicopter breaks the quietude of the morning. Up on the rock, Kevin begins to do a hippie shuffle, dancing with the hiking poles like a baton twirler.

The Black Hawk appears overhead with a deafening roar. It takes a bead on us and pauses about 100 feet up. The rotor wash nearly knocks us off our feet and bends the trees in an insta-hurricane. All the short evergreens around us bow as if in homage to its awesome power.

The tarp wrapping the patient whips at her face, and I worry that she'll get whapped with a grommet, so I move over and grab it to keep it from hitting her. She smiles.

We look up and see a small figure leaving the bird above us, slowly descending on a cable. As it gets closer, I see a long blond braid hanging from a black helmet onto the shoulder of a green flight suit. The medic gets pulled into the trees but simply pushes off against them in a gradual descent toward Rescue Rock. I think of the power of these machines and marvel at how nonchalant the medic is. *Probably used to getting shot at,* I say to myself—the Guard's members do this in war zones. This is nothing. Peaceful LZ, sunny day, raw beauty all around.

I'm standing with the patient when the medic hits the ground, unhooks, and walks over. A hand lifts the visor, and I see a petite young woman striking like a Viking. She talks to the patient for a moment, leaning in close because of the thunder from above, and then looks up as a litter comes out the open door of the Black Hawk. A rope dangles beneath it, and the medic grabs the rope and steers the spinning basket away from the trees to a small open spot in front of the patient. She's good. We help the patient into the litter, strapping her in and covering her face to protect her from the tree branches on the way up. Her husband gives her a kiss and she flies aloft, inching her way to the side of the copter.

As the medic hooks back in, she hands me a Helitack bag full of the rope she used to guide the litter. "Will you bring this back to me?" she asks over the whir of the rotors, standing close and staring me in the eyes.

"Of course." I clutch the big orange rope bag to my chest.

She smiles, drops her visor, and begins to levitate, like the Valkyries of Norse legend, her feet gently leaving the ground, her blond ponytail swept up into the sunlight. I shade my eyes with my hand and watch as, a minute later, her tiny frame slides into the helicopter, the crew waves, and the bird lifts off.

As I turn to gather gear in the morning sun, I wonder if we'll ever hear about what becomes of our patient.

CHAPTER 5

BAXTER PARK IS BIG, AS MANY OF OUR VISITORS FIND TO THEIR chagrin. Everything here is writ large. As state parks go, the place is massive, home to some of the most remote and rugged country left standing east of the Mississippi. At more than 209,000 acres, it's about one-fifth the size of Rhode Island. From the West Branch lands, along the Penobscot River, to giant Matagamon Lake in the north, it's about 50 miles as the eagle flies. With our 20-MPH speed limit, the journey through the park by car takes a couple of hours. On foot it takes days.

Governor Baxter's namesake park eclipses about half of the *national* parks in size. (Yeah, we're looking at you, Acadia.) However, it's a far cry from Wrangell–St. Elias, the largest national park at more than 8.3 million acres. That Alaska wildland is bigger than the states of Massachusetts, Maryland, Hawaii, Vermont, New Jersey, and New Hampshire and encompasses more acreage than Connecticut, Delaware, and Rhode Island combined. Gates of the Arctic and Denali national parks are not far behind. (The smallest national park, incidentally, is Gateway Arch in Missouri, which is a wee 90 acres.) All told, the national parks cover more than 52 million acres, or about 2 percent of the land mass of the United States.

Baxter sprawls across more landscape than famous national parks like Crater Lake, Zion, Redwood, Shenandoah, White Sands, Arches, Mesa Verde, and many more. Acadia, Maine's only member of this club, fits in Baxter's boundaries four times over. Baxter's neighboring national monument, Katahdin Woods and Waters, is about 42 percent of its size. The next largest recreational area in the Pine Tree State is Allagash Wilderness Waterway, which is roughly half the size of Acadia.

All together, the country's 6,600 state parks cover roughly 14 million acres. Alaska's state parks make up 3.4 million of those, with California's and New York's parks coming in second and third, respectively. Those three states account for almost half of all state park acreage. Alaska's Wood-Tikchik State Park is the largest, at more than 1.6 million acres. Baxter has the most land donated by a single individual.

Yet not one of these recreational areas spread across North America is quite the same as Baxter State Park.

And this was very much intentional.

Percival Proctor Baxter began to imagine this place about one hundred years ago. He actually started thinking about it many years before that, but he got serious in 1920. In the summer of that year the 44-year-old Portland native ventured to Katahdin with a hiking party of Maine luminaries, including a congressman, the state's fish and game commissioner, the chief game warden, and a host of journalists. At the head, hiking point, was the legendary warden and Chimney Pond resident, Roy Dudley.

It was the centennial of Maine's entry into the Union, and Baxter wanted to celebrate with a trip to one of the Pine Tree State's finest features. The scion of a prominent Forest City family—his father was a six-term mayor of Portland—Percival Baxter was a member of Maine's House of Representatives at the time, and he was convinced that the woods around Katahdin should be preserved in their wild state for Maine's people.

He wasn't alone in the thought.

Back in 1895, when sportsmen and nature lovers began to pour north to explore the state's woods, spurred on by Maine's first registered guide, Cornelia "Fly Rod" Crosby, the Maine Hotel Proprietors Association proposed the creation of a 900-square-mile park around Katahdin and Moosehead Lake. The Maine Sportsman's Fish and Game Association echoed that sentiment a year later, followed by the Maine Federation of Women's Clubs.

In 1910 and 1913, Congressman Frank Guernsey of Dover-Foxcroft introduced federal legislation to create a national park centered on the state's tallest peak, which Baxter vehemently opposed. He didn't like the idea of federal interference in these wild lands. Similar things were happening down in the Bar Harbor area, where rusticators began to make donations of land to stave off development and to preserve their idyllic getaway on Mount Desert.

Around the turn of the twentieth century, preservation of wild places was at the forefront of the national conversation, thanks to enlightened folks like Henry David Thoreau and Theodore Roosevelt, both of whom had experienced epiphanies on the slopes of Katahdin. Although Thoreau made his fame with the publication of *Walden*, he exerted a huge influence on a burgeoning environmental movement with his chronicle of visits to Maine's North Woods.

Thoreau wrote rapturously about the power of nature, and his quote "In wilderness is the preservation of the world" became a mantra for advocates of wild spaces. His only real *wilderness* adventure, though, came at Katahdin, where he was struck by the rawness and realness of a place where humans had yet to spread their dominion. He found these woods very wild and almost too real.

A few decades later, Katahdin also left a massive mark on the young Theodore Roosevelt, who climbed with his guide, Bill Sewall, in 1879. Just coming in to manhood, not long after the devastating death of his father, the sickly college student took heart from the fact that he was able to make it to the summit while all the other New Yorkers in his party could not. This even after losing his boots in Wassataquoik Stream and having to make the ascent in thin leather moccasins.

The feat proved something to Roosevelt, who, like many urban dwellers of the time, worried that he was becoming too soft and "European." After the climb, he wrote in his diary, "I can endure fatigue and hardship pretty nearly as well as these lumbermen." It was a pivotal moment in the personal history of the future 26th president.

Like Roosevelt, Percival Baxter first visited the woods at the base of Katahdin after attending Harvard, and he spent days fishing for trout with his father at the sporting camps on Kidney Pond in 1903. These log cabins sit in a line along the shore of the bean-shaped basin, with Katahdin rising dramatically out of the moose marsh at the pond's edge, surrounded by the other peaks of the Nesowadnehunk Valley. Almost a dozen trout ponds and streams were within an easy hike, making the region a world-class fishery. The young Baxter was swept away by the romance of the place.

In 1917, when he entered the Maine House of Representatives, Percival Baxter began to plan a park at the base of the mountain, crafting a bill in 1919 to buy 15,000 acres of what he considered the most beautiful landscape in the state. Editorial boards, sporting clubs, game commissioners, and conservationists of all stripes were on board. But his fellow legislators were not, and the bill died.

Which was why Baxter was back in these woods in early August 1920. He wanted to scale the mountain and to create a public relations campaign around a "Centennial Park at Katahdin" that would win the support of the people. That visit, which saw him crawling across the Knife Edge on his hands and knees, as so many have before and since, hardened his resolve like Katahdin granite. He wrote: "While I was there that day, I said to myself, 'This shall belong to Maine if I live.'"

When, as governor, he couldn't convince the Maine legislature to buy into his vision and release funds to purchase the great stone edifice, he did it himself. He said in a 1921 speech: "Maine is famous for its twenty-five hundred miles of seacoast, with its countless islands; for its myriad lakes and ponds; and for its forests and rivers. But Mount Katahdin Park will be the state's crowning glory, a worthy memorial to commemorate the end of the first and the beginning of the second century of Maine's statehood. This park will prove a blessing to those who follow us, and they will see that we built for them more wisely than our forefathers did for us."

He used his own funds to acquire the mountain and surrounding woods from Great Northern Paper, gifting the first 6,000 acres to the people of Maine in 1931. He continued his quest to build Baxter State Park across the next 30 years, securing large plots of land in a checkerboard pattern, even if he didn't own the connecting forests.

His second purchase was eight years later and miles away—the beautiful, mountainous country around South Branch Pond, an hour and a half from Katahdin on the park's tote road. It wasn't until the mid-1940s that Baxter got his hands on the parcels adjacent to the mountain. In 1945, he bought the land where my current duty station sits.

This was all in the future when he scaled Katahdin for his first and only time. As he stood on the peak that would one day bear his name, Baxter is said to have confided to his companions: "I wouldn't go through that experience again if someone offered me a million dollars. But I wouldn't have missed this wonderful scenic view for a million. This is the hardest thing I ever undertook."

———————

Baxter State Park is unique for a wide variety of reasons, foremost among them the governing structure that Percival Baxter established with his deeds of trust. Baxter famously gave the park to the people of Maine, but it's a state park in name only. It is not considered part of the state park system, and it takes no money from the state, funded by a trust that the very foresighted Percival Baxter left, camping fees, and sales of wood from the Scientific Forestry Management Area. In fact, even though my paycheck comes from Augusta, Baxter is quasi-private.

Nomenclature is the one area where I wish things had gone differently. Because of the name, we see a fair number of newbies who equate Baxter State Park with the state parks with which they're more familiar, like, say, Sebago Lake State Park, where you show up with coolers of beer to lie about and party. I wonder if it would be the same if the big brown sign out front read Baxter Wilderness or Baxter Nature Preserve, which would be more representative of the experience to be found within these bounds. But the name seemed logical when the park was founded, seven years before Aroostook State Park became the first actual Maine state park.

Baxter set up an unusual board to govern his new park, too. Like most other parks, we have a director, the highest-ranking on-staff member, but the real bosses are the three state officials who compose the Baxter State Park Authority: the Maine attorney general, the commissioner of the Department of Inland Fisheries and Wildlife, and the director of the Maine Forest Service. Baxter thought these public servants would protect the park from the ever-questing fingers of politics.

What truly sets Baxter Park apart, however, more than its size, funding, or leadership, is that it is a nature sanctuary first and foremost. Here, wildlife has dominion. Preservation is the primary goal, and human recreation is a far-distant second. We manage these wild lands for Bambi, not for the hunters.

While the national parks launch extensive ad campaigns, imploring people to visit, like their 2015 "Find Your Park" centennial promotion with major corporate sponsors, Baxter is not allowed to advertise. In fact, rather than encourage massive use, we *limit* entry, using parking spaces to regulate numbers. We routinely close Katahdin, the park's biggest draw, to protect sensitive vegetation—some of which grows nowhere else on the planet—from being trodden and trampled by thousands of soles. Limiting traffic also enhances the visitor experience. In many places, hikers have the trails to themselves, enjoying the kind of quietude and serenity rarely found these days, and this is one of the park's primary draws.

The idea that we give animals dominion really rankles some humans, contrasting as it does with centuries of human history. But it's why Baxter Park is a special place. It takes about four minutes of exploring online to find folks who think we're all a bit too zealous about this stuff. Many people expect Baxter Park to behave like other state parks, and online forums are filled with people bemoaning that Baxter is "overregulated." In other words, "I couldn't get in when I wanted to hike."

If you comb through our rules and regs, however, they're very much like those of most other parks. We ask that you don't litter, be careful with fire, show courtesy to other visitors, don't blast a radio. Not sure where the overregulation notion comes from, other than the fact that we limit access and ask people to camp in designated sites to preserve the wilderness experience that they came for in the first place.

I frequently get asked by friends and neighbors why I drive 3.5 hours to be a ranger in the woods around Katahdin. "Why don't you just work at Camden Hills State Park if you want to be a ranger?"

That green and lovely 5,700-acre recreation area, a place of high hills and ocean views, is only 25 minutes from my doorstep. It's Maine's second-largest state park, and I enjoy hiking Maiden Cliff and Bald Mountain in the off-season. But I always say the same thing: "Because I want to, you know, be a park ranger." I don't want to show RVs where to park. Or give tourists directions to the Farnsworth Museum in Rockland. Or recommend restaurants in Camden.

———

I have wanted to be a park ranger since I was 5, when I told my older sister that was the job for me.

"I thought you wanted to be a writer," she said.

"I do," I said, "but now a park ranger, too."

I don't know where the inspiration came from or why. For most of the other things I wanted to do when I grew up, the source was obvious. I wanted to play drums in a band because of the Monkees, who lived in a beach house, laughed all the time, and got all the girls. (At age 10, I got into a long, involved argument with my sister and brother, five and six years older and wiser, about why the Monkees were better than the Beatles.)

The writing life appealed because I was an avid reader from age 4 and somehow gleaned the notion that writers were their own bosses and didn't work on anyone else's schedule. With an overbearing father who regularly woke me at 6 A.M. to go split firewood or to work on one of his many projects, I was very keen on this idea. My sister and I used to cringe and hide whenever we heard his chain saw growl to life because we knew our day of fun had just ended.

Playing soccer professionally was another lifelong dream. (I still think I have something to offer certain clubs.) Unlike other kids in the late '70s who wore the T-shirt with the dribbling stick figure but seemed to care more about baseball or basketball, I actually watched soccer on TV whenever possible, which in the United States at that time meant very rare *Soccer Made in Germany* airings on PBS. I carefully cataloged moves, patterns of play, and who wore which boots. I obsessively read and reread my digest-size *Soccer America* magazines and borrowed whatever books I could find in the library, from Pele's fine memoir *My Life and the Beautiful Game* to Shep Messing's more apropos *The Education of an American Soccer Player*. I wore Umbro shirts and Adidas Sambas and willed my hair to grow longer, like Kevin Keegan's. One year for my birthday, my mom took me to see the New England Tea Men of the old North American Soccer League at our local Schaefer Stadium, and it was amazing. I didn't notice the largely empty stands or the artificial surface; I just saw Kevin "Cat" Keelan, on loan from England's Norwich City, making unbelievable saves and Mike Flanagan hammering away at the opponent's goal.

I also wanted—and this was a big one—to be a paramedic firefighter because of Johnny and Roy of Squad 51. I tuned in to every episode of the hit show *Emergency!*, wrestling with the rabbit ears on our huge wooden console TV until I could make out the contours of Los Angeles' Rampart region and get a good look at Dixie, the beautiful take-charge nurse. I had the action figures and the little red fire helmet and could think of nothing more noble than rescuing people from certain doom.

To my young, capital R romantic, grade-school way of thinking, firefighters were the logical extension of knights, with turnout coats and helmets for armor and axes for doing battle with a fearsome enemy. Plus, Johnny and Roy got all the girls, and the firehouse was filled with laughs. I harbored the desire to join the brotherhood of firefighters up through school. I remember the apprentice firefighters in my high school jumping the fences to get to the nearby station when the alarm rang, but I never got up the courage to join them, mostly due to my own shyness and insecurities. The other kids at Greely High School did not share my sense of cool, looking down at these young first responders. I didn't get over my hang-ups until the late '90s, at which point I decided to volunteer at my local department. The guys there didn't think I was cool until the night I literally bled for the cause, almost losing a finger in a late-night accident.

The duties of firefighters and park rangers do sometimes overlap—we fight wildland fires and rescue people in distress—and the inspiration for my ranger fixation might also have had something to do with *Emergency!* Very late in the show's run, Johnny and Roy are sent to a California national park to train the rangers in emergency medicine, resulting in the spin-off NBC show *Sierra*. I only discovered this recently, via YouTube, but there's an off chance I saw it when I was a kid. Built on the same premise as *Emergency!*, with rangers always busy on the kind of rescues we actually have maybe once a year, *Sierra* was also a Jack Webb production. It lasted a single season in 1974, despite its John Denver theme song and appearances by such future stars as Sharon Gless. I would have been 5 during its run, so it's possible I saw it at an impressionable young age but I doubt it.

Beyond that, most of the depictions of rangers in pop culture were more goofy than noble, like Ranger Smith in Yogi Bear cartoons, so I don't think TV was a big inspiration. Maybe I saw someone in uniform at a campground and was informed that living and working in a park was an occupational choice? Also possible, considering how much camping my family did. But there's no way to be sure.

———

Thinking back now, though, my interest in becoming an outdoors professional makes a whole lot of sense. Being outside, away from society's boxes—houses, offices, square living—was always for me. Growing up, I had a treehouse in a big old pine, a few mismatched boards forming a platform 15 or so feet off the pine needle floor. My parents used the 2 acres of our backyard as a babysitter, and I was always encouraged—and by that I mean ordered under penalty of death—to "go outside and play."

When I wasn't running in the woods, I was reading through all of the historical fiction stories about the French and Indian War and the

American Revolution that my middle school library had. I can't recall titles or authors, but I can picture the musty old hardcovers. They were written expressly for kids, and many took place almost exclusively in the woods. The natives, the mountain men, the soldiers—they all lived in the forest. Even when I graduated to fantasy books, like *The Hobbit* or *The Sword of Shannara*, the protagonists were always questing through the woods and camping under a canopy of trees. The woods were the backdrop to my life, both literally and culturally.

For me, there was no better place than a tent. Somehow, those nylon walls were the antithesis of square life, synonymous with adventure. When you wake up and unzip the flap of a tent, it's almost like opening a magic portal: you know you'll be stepping out to explore someplace exciting.

My family were avid campers. We never traveled much outside of New England, but we spent at least a couple of weeks in a tent somewhere a few times every year. My favorite places in the world were where we tented. The whole family got along, my father's hypertension relaxed a few points, and my brother and sister had no real options but to pay attention to me, at least a little.

I fell in love for the first time in a tent. She was a pony-tailed blond, a radiant woodland angel I met while at New Hampshire's Pawtuckaway State Park. Her family's site was near our family's, and we spent the entire time together. She was 12, I was 5—we worked it out. When she left, I was devastated, retreating to my tent to cry, an event that has become part of family lore.

My first kiss was in a tent. Set up in the yard of my cousin's neighbor, the fabric walls provided just the sort of privacy a nervous tween needed. (We spent a while in there until I really got the hang of it.)

I experienced my first serious hanky-panky a few years later atop a sleeping bag in a different tent with a different girl, trying to be as quiet as possible, so as not to get found out. A high school girlfriend and I used to hop the fence at a local state park and hang out after dark for similar reasons.

My wife and I spent a lot of our formative time together in tents. I proposed to her with a gumball-machine ring at our favorite camping spot, kneeling on the granite rocks along the shore. When we got married the following year, we celebrated in a tent set up in a very similar spot—a big open field on the salt water.

I must have seen rangers on these trips. During the summer between my junior and senior years in high school, I remember visiting a nearby state historic site, an old bastion on Pemaquid Bay, with my girlfriend at the time, who was a college sophomore. Though both of us had outsized intellectual curiosity, we were there more for the opportunity to go parking than to learn anything. When we arrived, a young woman, in ranger brown and green, was closing up for the day.

"That would be a cool gig," I said, and my hipster girlfriend, who longed for the city, looked at me like I was infirm.

This was a common reaction among my friends—a complete disinterest in the outdoors and the "hicks" who lived there—and I had a difficult time intellectually reconciling my love for the woods with the other aspects of my personality. I came up a punk rocker, a fan of the Beats, and wanted to play in indie rock bands and tour the nation in an Econoline van, traveling city to city, like a New Wave Kerouac. Or play soccer, traveling from historic metropolis to venerable burg, preferably in Europe. Or work somewhere as a full-time firefighter/paramedic, living in a downtown station and writing when off duty. Or whiling away the days as an expat, like Henry Miller, in some exotic hot spot, penning books with a zaftig muse. Despite my love for the outdoors, it always seemed metropolitan life was for me, and I gave my parents endless grief when we moved to a little village of 500 in Maine's Mid-Coast region.

My mom laughs that her depressed, long-haired, punk rock teenager, who talked about how badly he wanted to hit the city with its lights and vibrancy and music and girls and ideas, is the same guy who now happily cleans toilets in a wilderness area, population 50 on a busy day. Shortly after moving to an actual city, I found it *wasn't* really for me.

College took me to Worcester, Massachusetts. While there, punk rock sent me to Boston and to Providence, Rhode Island. Visits to friends and family took me to Philadelphia and to Washington, DC.

For me, all these cities suffered from—as one backcountry sage once put it—"too many hogs for the teat." I discovered I'm more comfortable in places with fewer people. I don't have the patience to wait in lines; I'm too shy for the zillions of weekly personal interactions; I miss the natural beauty and quietude. I often feel the world is too much with me when I'm surrounded by tens of thousands of other humans.

Plus, a new development had begun to percolate when I graduated from college, bringing just about everything I liked about the city right into my house. Thanks to a modem, I didn't have to travel to Kenmore Square to go to Nuggets and Planet Records to get those rare Neutral Milk Hotel bootlegs. Or visit the Harvard Coop for thumbed-through copies from City Lights Books. I could have them sent to me. The internet made the urban jungle, which I didn't much like anyway, seem all the more unnecessary.

My band made records and I played festivals in New York, but one day I came to the conclusion that I'd rather be a park ranger than a punk rocker.

Ironically, it was a favorite of the sophisticates who gave me permission to do so. Jack Kerouac's *The Dharma Bums* awakened me to the fact that hipsters and woodlands need not be mutually exclusive.

The book chronicles the mountain-climbing adventures and quest for enlightenment of poet Japhy Ryder (the real Gary Snyder) and Ray Smith (Kerouac) as they bounce between the city and the woods. They were neither square nor chawbacon, but rather cool dudes for whom the outdoors was a vibrant, intellectually stimulating escape.

Born in the industrial city of Lowell, Massachusetts, Kerouac wrestled with the same urban/wild dilemma as me, working for the U.S. Forest Service as a fire lookout a year before the publication of *On the Road* changed his life.

And then, of course, there was Cactus Ed. I discovered Edward Abbey's *Desert Solitaire* after college, and it, too, resonated with me. Here was an erudite deep thinker who preferred the society of jackrabbits and didn't have much use for city dwellers. For me, Abbey was similar to Kerouac in that he was a countercultural icon who did things his own way. A writer and a ranger. That was about as cool as cool gets.

Closer to home, I became a fan of Helen and Scott Nearing, who helped inspire the back-to-the-land movement with their book *The Good Life*. A radical economist, Scott Nearing was an early advocate of simple living and getting back to what's real, and the couple's idea of the good life resonated with my office-bound self.

While I was absorbing all this, I worked and lived in a city—albeit a tiny one, Hallowell, Maine. My girlfriend (now my wife) and I had an apartment there for a short time, and we decided downtown dwelling, with its traffic noise, smoky downstairs neighbors, and close confines, was not for us.

We made it a couple of years before running to the country, setting up in the wing of a barn in Bowdoinham, next door to the painter Carlo Pittore. But I still commuted to Portland for work as a writer. That was after a year at *Maine Times* in Topsham, where I worked alongside the paper's resident wild man, Andrew Weegar, the outdoor writer and Maine guide, who I thought had about the most interesting lifestyle ever.

Eventually my girlfriend and I landed near the coast, and I took a job in the Camden–Rockport area as a magazine editor. I was lucky enough to be that glossy regional's outdoor guy, which meant exploring Maine's wild places and reporting back. We spent a fair amount of time each year— probably months—in a tent, either on assignment or just escaping for a long weekend or a backpack trip.

The magazine sent me to do several stories in Baxter State Park, a place I was already in love with. I had first visited on a climbing trip with uncles and cousins when I was 10, and my family spent many nights at South Branch Pond. I shared this magnificent wild land with my future wife when we first started dating.

Hanging out with rangers, it began to become clear to me that I belonged there with them more than I did back in my corner office in a touristy "ruburb." Even after my wife and I settled in Appleton, a town in a rolling valley on the St. George River, where the Camden Hills finally peter out, I felt too suburban, too plugged in to the digital hive mind.

On one of those Baxter trips, legendary backcountry ranger Brendan Curran told me he always found it funny that when people packed up their campsite to go home, they often said, "Time to go back to the real world." As if, he chuckled, the places they were returning to, with climate control at the touch of a button, reality TV, and all kinds of digital connectivity, were somehow more real than the rocks and roots of Baxter Park, where you have to worry about life-sustaining things like water and weather and food.

This prompted me to recall a discussion I had with one of my wife's friends, who wondered why we moved to rural Maine. "Because it's real," I told her, in contrast to the suburbs with their rows of identical, plastic-sided houses and Jonesing (as in "keeping up with the") residents with their posturing affectations. Whenever I went to Baxter, I felt myself rewilding.

In 2001, I suggested to my editor in chief that we do a story on dream jobs in Maine, because at the magazine we heard from countless people who said they'd move Down East on the next tide if they only had a way to make a living. The first vocation that came to my mind was Baxter State Park ranger. I interviewed Stewart Guay, who at the time held the enviable post as an alpine ranger at Chimney Pond, the spectacular 3-acre tarn sitting halfway up Katahdin.

Guay explained that, growing up in New Hampshire, his boyhood dream, too, was to be a park ranger. Unlike me, he went to an outdoorsy school, Paul Smith's College in the Adirondacks, and after graduation set right out to find a park to work in, landing at Baxter in the '90s.

It would take me a few more years to reach the same conclusion.

CHAPTER 6

I DIDN'T KNOW MUCH ABOUT THE HISTORY OF PARK RANGERS WHEN I decided to become one. I just wanted to live a life like Ranger Brendan Curran's, camping in cabins deep in the woods, rescuing people, fighting forest fires, and flying around in army-green Hueys. I would discover that the profession has a storied history, reaching at least as far back as medieval England.

The word *ranger* appears to come from the Latin word *regardatores*, which means those who regard, or inspect, the forest; and in knightly times, that's just what certain crown officials did. They would "range" through the king's forest, protecting the royal deer from poachers. Because they were the only law enforcement around, they also often ended up ensuring that people followed regulations in the woods and outlands.

Historical English letters refer to the commissioning of a ranger as far back as 1341. About a century later, official paperwork in the Rolls of Parliament mentions "all manner and singular offices of Foresters and Rangers of our said Forests."

In the American colonies, British rangers were soldiers comfortable in the outdoors who covered vast territory between forts, monitoring the movement of natives and French troops. They served as scouts and guides and led reconnaissance patrols through the vast Appalachian woodland. During the French and Indian War, members of one of the best-known outfits, Roger's Rangers, distinguished themselves as an early commando team, capable of hitting the French hard and fast in remote locations. Some historians consider these rangers the country's first special forces operators.

Decades later, General George Washington planted the seeds of today's U.S. Army Rangers when he ordered Lieutenant Colonel Thomas Knowlton to create a group of elite reconnaissance patrollers (he'd already rejected the services of Rogers, thinking him a spy). The team became known as Knowlton's Rangers and was the nation's first official ranger unit.

When two new national parks—Yellowstone and Yosemite—were created in the years after the Civil War, U.S. Army personnel were assigned to protect them from poachers. In 1883, the United States passed legislation that increased staffing in parks and outlawed hunting and trapping. It also allowed the secretary of the interior to request help patrolling the parks from the secretary of war. Thus, U.S. Cavalry soldiers rode into Yellowstone in 1886 to protect and preserve the park from game thieves and other despoilers. They remained until 1918.

These mounted units became known as rangers, and their large, wide-brimmed hats became the familiar Smokey the Bear or Montana campaign hats that modern National Park Service rangers are forced to wear. (Thanks be, we are not required to wear these big service hats outside formal occasions and instead are issued baseball caps.)

The first officially appointed park ranger, an individual whose sole responsibility was to preserve and protect a national park, is an honor that goes to one of two men. Galen Clark was commissioned on May 21, 1866 to patrol Yosemite and worked at the role for more than 24 years. Harry Yount served as a gamekeeper in Yellowstone in the 1880s. Because there remains debate about which of these two towering national park anchors—Yellowstone and Yosemite—came first, historians remain unsure if Clark or Yount was the first ranger.

What isn't in doubt is that after his first season in 1880, Yount thought it wise to create a "small, active reliable police force ... [to] assist the superintendent of the park in enforcing laws, rules, and regulations." That suggestion appeared to reach unsympathetic ears, because it wasn't until September 1898 that Charles A. Leidig and Archie O. Leonard became the first permanently appointed rangers in a national park, taking up residence at Yosemite. Presumably they were among the first to receive the badges that read "Forest Reserve Ranger," used between 1898 and 1906 by the rangers of the U.S. Department of the Interior.

Rangers have been doing the business ever since. Even former president Gerald Ford got into the fun, spending a season at Yellowstone in 1936. (He is the only U.S. president to have served as a park ranger.)

———

Baxter State Park's first ranger is widely held to be Richard Holmes, who began working for "Mr. Baxter" in 1939. A new graduate of the University of Maine's prestigious forestry program, the 23-year-old was most certainly the park's first seasonal ranger.

Holmes visited the newly created park to ski and adventure on the slopes of Katahdin in the winter of 1938. When he was making arrangements to stay at the Forest Service's cabin on Chimney Pond, he was told that officials were looking to hire someone to work in the park the next summer. "I wanted that job," he told a reporter later. And he meant to have it—so much so that immediately upon returning home from his winter trip, the Northeast Harbor native went to see each of the three members of the Baxter State Park Authority to lobby for the position. He then visited former governor Percival Baxter at home.

Baxter asked the young college student what kind of outdoor experience he had and was suitably impressed. Holmes got the job, which paid about $100 a month, as he recalled later.

In June, Richard Holmes steered his 1929 Model A Ford toward Katahdin, bumping along the old tote road from Millinocket to Togue Pond. He was struck by the woodsy bonhomie of the handful of residents who lived in this forest beneath the mountain. These included John O'Connell, a retired papermaker, who, along with his wife, made beds out of pine boughs and sold them to tourists for a quarter.

Holmes set up a "ranger station" at Katahdin Stream Campground in the form of a 10-by-12-foot canvas wall tent. He dug a hole to bury his food. He was given no uniform, no vehicle, and no badge. In fact, the only equipment he was issued was a Pulaski, the woodland firefighter's main weapon, which combines an ax head with a grub hoe. This was for clearing brush around the campground.

The eager new ranger spent his summer cutting blowdowns and snags on the trails, keeping the campground, and watching for wildfires. He was also charged with orienting and assisting the 10,000 visitors who hiked and camped in the park that summer. Only 10,000 of them to check in all by himself.

Over a campfire, Holmes cooked and heated water for bathing and warmed his tent with a sheet-metal stove as temperatures began falling in September. When an October snowstorm dropped more than a foot, he moved into a cabin at nearby Daicey Pond at the invitation of the Yorks, a couple who ran a sporting camp on the scenic basin.

The most exciting event in the park that summer was the disappearance of Donn Fendler, a 12-year-old boy from Rye, New York. Holmes received an alert on July 17 that Fendler had not returned with his family from a hike up Katahdin. The ranger and five volunteers started off on the Hunt Trail at 7 o'clock that night to begin a hasty search.

They saw no sign of the boy on the trail or on the wide expanse of the Tableland, so they descended down the Saddle Trail to Chimney Pond. Not finding him on that popular route, they returned to the summit and trekked back down the Hunt Trail to Katahdin Stream to get some sleep before resuming the search the next day.

Holmes was involved for several of the nine days of the search, which made news all across the country, before Fendler was found alive and uninjured 8 miles away on the East Branch of the Penobscot River.

Richard Holmes worked in Baxter Park only that one summer before leaving to begin a career in surveying. He would put his outdoor skills to good use in the Rocky Mountains, teaching arctic survival skills to servicemen in the Army Air Corps during World War II.

Like Richard Holmes, I really wanted to work at Baxter Park. My childhood aspirations never subsided. When I interviewed the park naturalist, Jean Hoekwater, for a 1999 profile in *Down East* magazine, I asked her how one gets hired as a ranger at the park. She recommended I put in an application. I naively wrote a letter to the park director offering my services, and he wrote back that I should apply. So I did. And waited.

Meanwhile, I sat at my desk at the magazine, watching the fish hawks outside my office window as they circled below the clouds, wild and free. At that point I was managing editor, with a private corner office in a beautiful, old Victorian cottage just a short walk from Penobscot Bay. I had everything an aspiring writer should want: a high-profile position at a beloved institution; an audience that numbered in the hundreds of thousands; a group of talented colleagues whom I admired. I got to interview the most interesting people in the state, stay at the finest inns, and eat at the best restaurants. But I was miserable. I felt confined in a box. Which was why I envied the ospreys, which lived on their own schedules and could roam wherever they wanted.

So, one May day, I decided to quit.

Steeped in the New England compunction of not wanting to disappoint, I dreaded the conversation ahead as I climbed the stairs to the executive level and knocked on the door of the editor in chief. He was about the same age as my father, a smart guy who instinctively knew how to run a magazine and manage people. In his tweed jacket and horn-rims, he looked like an English professor. I learned a lot from his red pen, and we always got along well.

"Remember when we did the dream jobs story in the 'Making a Living in Maine' issue?" I asked him.

He nodded.

"Well, I'm leaving to take a job as a Baxter Park ranger."

He was disappointed but not overly surprised. He knew I was never happier than when I was off on assignment in the backcountry. He'd sent me to the park countless times: to write pieces on Gabe and Marcia Williamson, the inspirational rangers at Daicey Pond, on the park naturalist, on Russell and Davis ponds, on climbing Katahdin in the winter. When I had talked to him about my raise a few months earlier—pissed that it was dramatically lower than those of some of my colleagues—he told me I got less because I "didn't seem very happy."

I *wasn't* happy. I'd been at the "Magazine of Maine" for the better part of a decade, rising up the masthead from assistant to associate to managing editor. But now I felt in a rut, like I'd done all there was to do. I wanted to see a more contemporary design, harder-hitting pieces, less fluff. I was tired of lining the pockets of the owners. I was tired of listening to the editor in chief wax lyrical about one of the other editors, calling him the "best writer in Maine." I figured I could stay at *Down East* and continue interviewing the interesting people of the state—or I could go out and become one.

It went deeper than that, however. Ever the romantic, I didn't want to grow up to be simply a magazine editor. It struck me one day how many books I'd have to my name if I'd been generating word counts to that end instead of filling magazine pages. I found myself envious of other young writers who were publishing exciting titles to great reception.

One of the reasons I wanted to become a writer in the first place was the freedom it allowed, the ability to manage my own time—and to work at home in my underwear, if I wanted to. That seemed a completely alien concept to me now, sitting at a desk from 7:30 A.M. to 6 P.M. five days a week, wearing the tie I hated to put on. (My buddy Matthew Mayo called this required accessory the "Daily Noose.") As an introvert, I disliked interviewing and making cold calls and all the requisite small talk. I wasn't fond of placating advertisers or all those wannabe writers who sent us their unsolicited material.

And my issues extended beyond the workplace. The area had grown over the years, and it became impossible to make a left-hand turn out of the magazine's driveway during the summer, when Route 1 was thronged with tourists. Even Route 17 in my own neighborhood had begun to remind me of New Jersey on many mornings, with lines of cars headed toward the coast. This was probably caused by road work delays rather than tourists, but it didn't matter. There were too many hogs for the teat. I longed for the woods.

I felt stuck, like Luke Skywalker on Tatooine. I'd done everything right to that point—got a degree, followed it up with a good job. I'd been responsible right out of the gate (thanks to the indentured servitude of student loans), settled into a comfortable position, and worked exceptionally hard to climb the ranks. But I was not happy. Life was meant for living; otherwise what was the point?

I thought about the situation one of my father's college buddies found himself in: He left school and found work at a corporate law firm, a job he hated every single day of his life. But it paid an enormous salary, and he had a big house to maintain and two daughters to send to college, so he was always too scared to leave. I didn't want the same fate. There are too many carcinomas, wayward drivers on snowy roads, and unexpected heart conditions for that. (At least my own dad, festering as a vice president at a big Boston bank, decided he'd had enough of the cancerous growth of the suburbs and elected to move to Maine.)

Both my grandfathers died before they were 70. I did the math. At that point I was already half-cooked and felt dragged along on a train bound inexorably for a destination I did not want to arrive at. And I thought I had just enough courage to jump.

I talked with my wife, Lisa, about other avenues for scratching this adventure itch. One of my uncles was a U.S. Coast Guard commander and tried subtle recruiting at family campouts. While I never wanted to join the military to impose Reagan–Bush neocon order on faraway countries, I thought highly of the Coasties. They rescued people, enforced environmental laws, and ran drug interdiction against huge narco traffickers. That sounded like adventure. I got as far as the recruitment office. They seemed excited . . . to have a journalist like me at their Boston base. No chance of rescuing people. No Maine duty station. No thanks.

I considered going full time as a firefighter or maybe joining the Maine Warden Service. Lisa didn't like the sound of either of those. At least the ranger gig had a romance she could participate in, and she loved the place, too. The schedule seemed doable because she was working for a college program and was more able to take time off in the summer.

So I quit.

But not without reservation. Lisa was pregnant with our first child, and we had a mortgage to pay. Plus, as a fairly shy and introverted book nerd, could I handle everything a ranger had to deal with? Rescues? Bad guys?

I decided I wanted the challenge. I've always felt the need to test myself—to push beyond what's easy. Perhaps this is because my father's favorite saying was "Use your head for something besides a hat rack" and I questioned whether I was bright enough. Maybe it was because we moved a couple of times and I was "the new kid" or because I was a small and quiet kid and thus always had to prove my worth. I also felt a need for a simpler, quieter, more real life, to be on my own—like one of the ospreys outside my office window.

So I quit.

I could tell by the slump of my editor's shoulders that he understood the woods was where I belonged. We decided I would remain the magazine's editor at-large and continue handling several of the popular columns I wrote each month. At least I'd be able to pay the mortgage.

Within a few days of leaving *Down East*, I received a big box in the mail from Baxter Park. I went at it like a kid on his birthday, tearing at the packing tape, pulling back the cardboard flaps. It didn't emit glowing light or play cinematic music upon opening, but it might just as well have. Inside were my uniforms, brown and green and, to my mind, magic. On each shirt's left arm, the one that shows out a truck window, was an embroidered patch depicting Katahdin with *RANGER* written across the blue sky above it in arcing red letters. There were green baseball caps with emblems that read "To Preserve and Protect."

It got better. In a little plastic bag was a badge. Two inches tall, brass, weighty in my palm, it read "STATE OF MAINE, RANGER, BAXTER STATE PARK" and depicted items from the state flag: the pine tree, the farmer, the moose, and the mariner. After staring at it for a few minutes, I hollered for my wife to come look, like a toddler with the toy he always wanted.

I was a little surprised the park just sent out badges to anyone. Granted, I had made it through their hiring process, standing up before a panel of rangers and HR people, answering questions that were obviously written by committee. I was a Registered Maine Guide, which attested to the fact that I was at least somewhat capable outdoors, according to the Maine Warden Service. I'd been a volunteer firefighter for a few years, which meant I had some experience with rescue. I was certified in wilderness medicine. I'd even been involved in a litter carry on the Hunt Trail years before, joining a team of volunteers to help haul a woman with a knee injury down from the treeline. And the park staff surely had seen the many magazine articles I'd written about their realm, so they knew I knew my way around.

Even so, I had been a magazine writer and editor. Most of my professional life to that point was spent talking on the phone or typing on a keyboard. The guys at the fire department referred to me, not entirely in fun, as a desk jockey. I'm not sure I could have found a callus on my hands (maybe from playing guitar); my fingernails were gnawed.

They'd give a badge to someone like me? Could an introverted writer, more comfortable at home with a book than in just about any social situation, handle the weight of this uniform?

I was about to find out. I was to report in the first few days of May, just a couple of weeks away.

CHAPTER 7

I REPORTED FOR DUTY AT BAXTER STATE PARK HQ IN MAY 2002, WITH a handful of other new recruits. Headquarters, which I'd visited as a camper and again as a job candidate, was a typical state office except for the big wood-topped counter welcoming anyone who walked in. The vibe was far more official and orderly than that of the retrofitted Victorian cottage that housed my old office. The bathrooms were steel gray. The meeting room had folding chairs and wall paneling. I didn't know what to expect. I also didn't know any of the rangers milling around, so I looked at the scale model of Katahdin that sat off to one side.

I knew I was assigned to Katahdin Stream, one of the trailhead campgrounds at the base of the mountain. I'd met the ranger there a few years before when I'd camped down by the water with my wife. He was a surly redhead, five or six years older than me, with the trademark ranger baseball cap and a mustache. We thought he was a curmudgeonly character, scowling as we checked in, and assumed he didn't like us.

He didn't.

I had also spent some time with this ranger on the only park rescue I'd been involved in up to that point, which occurred in 1995 when I was visiting the Daicey Pond rangers to do a magazine profile. For the better part of an evening, Lisa and I helped carry a woman with a knee injury down Hunt Trail.

This guy ran the show on that long night, and he did an excellent job. As someone who sat through countless boring meetings in a boardroom, I'd grown to appreciate a strong leader.

He'd never seemed to recognize us on any of our subsequent visits to Katahdin Stream. Even so, I was pretty sure he didn't like me.

Robin Stevens, who now works my shift at Kidney Pond, told me she felt the same way when she first arrived to work at Togue Pond Gate. "I was so pissed when I found out he was the duty officer on my ten o'clock shift. He always seemed so grumpy."

Now we were partners. I was the new cadet at the Bruce White Ranger Academy, the informal training program at Katahdin Stream. I learned that Bruce put his new partners through their paces, and he'd had a lot of them. I wondered what happened to the last one.

As I was sweating all this that morning, a dark-haired, middle-aged woman came by to introduce herself. She was Helen White, a gatekeeper from the north end and, more important, the wife of my new partner.

Helen took me around and introduced me to Bob Howes, the always-smiling, gray-haired district ranger who'd been at the park for 30 years and would be my new boss while my actual boss finished up at the Maine Criminal Justice Academy. Next was Jodi Tollett Browning, a tall, red-headed law enforcement ranger. I remembered Bob from my interview and was pretty sure Jodi had been on that Hunt Trail rescue. A park staffer who looked a lot like her had told me that evening, as I ran out of water, that all the rangers dipped their Nalgene water bottles in the streams and drank untreated water so long as it was moving. I just wasn't supposed to tell anyone else.

Helen walked me around, holding on to my arm, and showed me where the meetings were held, where the all-important business offices that processed paychecks were upstairs, and how to find the mailboxes, introducing me to everyone we met along the way. Her kindness helped settle the new-job anxieties.

It was soon clear that people who got jobs at Baxter Park stayed for a long time. Each successive person I met seemed to have more years in. I did meet another probie for Roaring Brook and a couple of new gatekeepers, but it seemed most of the rangers had some seasons under their belts.

When Helen finally dropped me off with Bruce, he looked at me and shrugged. We started to collect supplies to load up Katahdin Stream's pickup and head in to the park. The battered blue Ford looked like it had seen many miles, and Bruce hated it, but I thought it was amazing simply because of the green stickers along its front end that read "Park Ranger."

"Let me get this straight," Bruce said as we stacked boxes into the bed. "You left a year-round job as an editor at *Down East* magazine to come work here?"

I nodded.

"A high-up, year-round position at *Down East*?"

"Yep."

"You're crazy." He shook his head in disbelief. "Mental."

"I couldn't take it there anymore. Always wanted to be a park ranger."

"Really?"

"Ever since I was a kid."

He told me of the difficulties he had trying to find work in the winter. Every winter. He'd done construction in Virginia. Carpentry in upstate New York. He'd worked as a lift operator at Sunday River and was a handyman at the Little Lyford camps. All so he could hang on to this park ranger gig.

He looked at me and shook his head again before hopping into the cab and turning on both the park radio and a country music radio station. These were constants and one bled into the other. We rode an hour into the park, and he explained how things worked. I was his assistant. He would run the campground, working on the A team—the weekend shift—while I performed the tasks he set out for me. He'd spend a couple of weeks working with me to make sure I understood the job before letting me loose on my own. This was reassuring. Somewhat.

"I've had to train a lot of people before you," he said. "Most of 'em didn't last long."

When we arrived at Katahdin Stream, he showed me my camp out behind the ranger station, hard by the babbling namesake waterway. It was a small two-room shack with a shower stall built into the bedroom. There was supposed to be hot running water, but it hadn't been hooked up yet. No toilet at all. The outhouse was across the parking lot. It was primitive, but I had assumed it would be worse.

"I kinda thought we'd live in wall tents or something," I said, thinking about Boy Scout camp.

"You really are crazy, college boy."

I had a blast those first few weeks, learning the business of rangering. Katahdin Stream is the park's oldest camping area, consisting of a wide field for picnicking with two arms on either side along the watercourse itself, where the tent sites and lean-tos are. On the first side of the stream are a handful of additional sites reached by foot, to which campers have to haul all their gear in from the parking area.

The ranger station itself, a run-down, stick-built structure made to look like a log cabin, with a screened-in porch running the length of the front, sat on the other side of a wide, 5-foot-deep pool created by a dam. Bruce and Helen lived in the quarters at the back of the ranger station: a bedroom, a kitchen, a living room, and a small bathroom with shower and toilet. The place got little natural light and opened onto the much-brighter ranger station office on one side and the porch on the other. A stone's throw away was a tiny shed that we used as a garage for tool storage.

We kept all the rescue supplies in a chicken wire cage at the back of the garage. As one of the major trailheads, Katahdin Stream has its own cache of emergency equipment, including hopeful stuff, like plastic boots for walk-downs—"You'll grow to love walk-downs," Bruce told me—and less hopeful stuff, like body bags. Supplies also include climbing ropes, blankets, MREs for multiday incidents that require easy food, and glow sticks for signaling helicopters. The same cage held our firefighting gear: helmets, a big orange Homelite fire pump, Pulaskis, fire rakes, and sundry other items that I thought were about the coolest collection of implements I'd ever seen. This despite the fact that they all looked well used and maybe handed down from World War II.

In the ranger station, we went over radio protocols. Baxter Park, like every workplace, has its own vernacular, and an intriguing one at that. I'd have to keep a lot of numbers straight. "You are Unit 5," Bruce told me, sitting behind the desk, next to the base radio. "I'm 67." He listed a handful of unit numbers I should know, from 50 (the park director) to 51 (the chief ranger) to 53 (our supervisor). It became pretty clear that the "Fives" were the important ones. Several of those Fives certainly thought so.

"Listening to the radio is mandatory. Responding is optional," Bruce said. I should keep everything I transmitted short and to the point. "Don't ask too many questions," he continued. "You can't just talk. Think about what you're going to say before you trigger the mic."

I watched and listened as he used the radio for most of the first few days. He was amused when one of the reservation clerks at headquarters dressed me down for reserving a site without asking whether it was available first. I had called a few minutes before, was told it was not booked, and neglected to ask when I called again. "You can't just assume," she scolded. "Someone might have taken it."

"I don't think she likes you," Bruce said, laughing his trademark, nasally laugh.

67 took me 2 miles down the road to Abol Campground, which was closely linked with Katahdin Stream—due to proximity and the fact that it was another major trailhead—and explained that I would likely be covering Abol occasionally. I might also be asked to respond to emergencies on the Abol Trail, so I should know where their rescue equipment was stashed. We poked around in the office and the garage, seeing how the place was laid out.

We also stopped at the Birches, our thru-hiker camp, and he showed me the lean-tos and raised tent platform where the Appalachian Trail hikers would stay when they started arriving in about a month. Bruce and another ranger had just finished building this new camping area—the idea was to give AT hikers their own place, removed from the regular campground—and the lean-tos had the golden glow of newly worked wood.

"Don't let them get away with anything," 67 said of the future visitors to this place. "Believe me, they will try."

We drove up to Foster Field, the group site 2 miles north for which the Katahdin Stream Ranger Station was responsible. "Three more outhouses here that need cleaning," Bruce told me, grabbing the sprayer out of the back of the truck. He looked me in the eye. "Every day."

I nodded.

"And don't think you're some kind of hero and do it without the green gloves. We all wear them."

I put on the green gloves and went elbows deep in the riser.

67 seemed a little surprised that I wasn't squeamish about the toilets. "I figured some fancy magazine editor wouldn't want to get his hands dirty," he said. I didn't mind. I recognized immediately that real park rangers cleaned outhouses, and I wanted to be a real park ranger.

The best one I possibly could be.

———

Driving around with Bruce those first couple of weeks, I detected a begrudging approval. We laughed a lot. He told me how he grew up in the park, spending summers with his uncle right there at Katahdin Stream. This uncle worked for the Maine Department of Transportation, which maintained the park road, and he had stayed in a little cabin that was no longer there. Bruce came up in summers to fish with him and explore the park.

Because of that uncle, whom the park administration held a grudge against, thanks to park/DOT politics, Bruce never got any of the full-time, year-round ranger jobs he applied for. This despite being, from what I could tell, good at everything required of a ranger: rescue, maintenance, chain sawing, even, I was to shocked to discover, public relations. Better than our bosses, the full-timers. Of course, there were some things that other rangers might have a slight advantage at, like using the backhoe. And Bruce's bulky frame definitely got in the way of rapid ascents of the mountain. But not by much. He could do it all. He didn't seem fazed by big drunks, people bleeding out, pushy people from away, all the problems that I knew would test my resolve. Despite his gruff exterior, I felt lucky to have been assigned as Bruce's partner, and I made it a point to learn as much as I possibly could.

Wherever we went in the park, this guy was revered, from Togue Pond in the south, where he brought treats for the gatekeepers, to the north gate, where he spent a lot of time because his wife worked there. All the graduates of the Bruce White Ranger Academy thought highly of him, too, evidenced by the fact that they often dropped by Katahdin Stream to ask advice, to visit, and to borrow tools and supplies, because Bruce had one of everything and was famous for hoarding little oddments that he knew would one day prove useful.

After three weeks, he still called me "college boy," but he added a new nickname: Evergreen.

Sam Raimi's *Spider-Man* movie had just come out, and I told Bruce there should be a park ranger superhero. One of my friends had taken to calling me Ranger Danger when she heard I was going to be working at Baxter Park, and I thought that could be the name of this new character. Bruce immediately replied, "With his sidekick Evergreen."

Ranger Danger would be a park ranger by day and an environmental crusader in green by night, protecting natural places from corporate despoilers.

"The archnemesis could be a guy called Round-Up," Bruce said, referring to the controversial herbicide. We came up with all kinds of additional baddies as we scrubbed outhouses, drove between campgrounds, and sat around the desk at night.

For the next few weeks, whenever I screwed up—forgetting to account for a map I sold or saying something backward on the radio—he'd say, in a long growl, "*Evergreen.*"

I had Friday nights off but had to be on duty Saturday mornings, so I often hung around with Bruce and did ride-alongs on his shifts as the weekenders hit. We'd catch people trying to sleep in their cars rather than in a site, find vehicles with different plates on the front and back, and tell rowdies to quiet down. Occasionally we'd hang at the station with the Friday night duty officer, an old-timer who often had his dinner at Katahdin Stream.

During one of these visits, this character told me to pull up the office mat in the Katahdin Stream Ranger Station and have a look underneath. I did so and saw a very conspicuous bullet hole in the floor. He explained that many years ago a raccoon had gotten in while he was away at head-quarters, so he took care of it when he returned. I could imagine the drama, and probable dismissal, that would ensue if any of us discharged a sidearm in a ranger station, but the '70s were different times.

Back then, rangers were cowboys. Most lived in the field. They had countless adventures before the 1990s, when the decision was made that year-round rangers could live at home rather than in the park.

Like many rangers of his generation, this veteran didn't like having to go to meetings at headquarters or do any of the paperwork his supervisors required—he wanted to be in the park, rangering. Everything else was an onerous pain in the ass. I can't imagine what these guys, most of whom retired within a few years of my arrival, would think of Zoom, Google Docs and Google Earth, inReach, iMessage, game cameras, and all of the other high-tech tools supervisory rangers now use to do the job.

———————

The boss decided I was ready to go it alone after a couple of weeks of train-ing at the Bruce White Ranger Academy. He'd often ride around with me on my shifts, despite the fact that he was off duty, just helping and hanging out. (I figured this might be an indication he didn't hate me.) He usually had a story about a rescue he'd done the night before. All the excitement seemed to happen on his watch, which made sense. He worked Friday and Saturday nights, when the most people were on the mountain. Nothing ever occurred during my Tuesday, Wednesday, and Thursday nights or Friday or Saturday mornings. But he'd hop into our truck and tell me how he'd rescued a U.S. Army Ranger trainer who was having a panic attack or called for a "jungle penetrator" up in the gnarly conifer scrub on the Owl. This device, which the National Guard's massive Sikorsky Black Hawk helicopters drop into dense bush to extract wounded soldiers, looks like an anchor and consists of two seats. I lived for the day I could have some of these adventures myself.

I came close only once during my two seasons at Katahdin Stream. I was cleaning the toilets at Foster Field, one of which was set back into the woods, a short walk from the truck. I had my handheld, a big, gray brick older than I was, probably dating back to Vietnam, in a holster on my belt. It sparked to life: "50–Katahdin Stream." The park director was looking for me. I was almost done scrubbing the riser and figured I'd call him back. A minute later it crackled again: "50–Abol." I made for the truck. It sounded like something might be up. "50–Abol." Just as I got into the truck and grabbed the mic, the Abol ranger picked up . . . and got the ride of a lifetime.

The park director sent the Abol ranger and a roving ranger after a hiker with a prosthetic lower leg. It attached at the knee, and the joint had swollen so much during his climb up the steep Abol Trail he could no longer keep the artificial appendage on. The two rangers quickly made their way to assist and helped him up to the Tableland, and they all flew off in a Black Hawk. Then 50 picked them up at the airport and treated them to dinner.

Now, it's extremely rare to get a helicopter ride. I've had a handful in eighteen years, but I know plenty of rangers who've never seen the inside of a helo. It's even more unusual to have that flight be with the Guard in a Black Hawk. All of mine have been with the Maine Forest Service, and most of them were practice runs during training sessions in the Forest Service's Bells. Only one was for business, and that was in a Huey during a forest fire. If I had run for the radio that day, I'd have been in luck. My belief in the sanctity of clean toilets was my downfall.

———

Clean toilets were important to my new boss, however. Bruce always seemed impressed that the busy hoppers at Katahdin Stream were well scrubbed and shiny when he returned for his Friday afternoon shift. I also managed to get all the things accomplished that he left for me, whether it be draw-shaving lean-to logs or putting away firewood. This despite the fact that I could barely read his left-handed scrawl and spent about half of my shift just trying to interpret what exactly it was he wanted done.

I could tell he was pleased with the way I handled myself checking in the campers and in the difficult interactions, too. There was the time a guy stepped up and screamed in my face because I told him he wasn't allowed to park in our walk-in parking to climb the mountain. The bearded fellow, a little taller than me, roared, "I drove all the way from Maryland to climb this mountain!"

"Well, you'll have to make better plans next time, sir," I said, holding my ground.

He blasted at me for a whole minute before he finally relented, slamming the door of his European sports car and turning toward the south exit, heading out rather than climbing one of our 45 other peaks, hiking any of the 200-some miles of trail, or paddling one of our 50 lakes and ponds.

Then there was the time during a Saturday morning shift when I told a middle-aged mom that she was going to have to relocate her tent to *this* side of the "No Tents Beyond This Point" sign at Foster Field. She'd elected to put it up about 15 yards into the woods. She didn't scream at me—just burst into sobs. She told me that nice little piece of forest was "the only thing good about this camping area with all the dust and the people driving by all the time." While I was sympathetic—Foster Field is right on Park Road—and tried to be as polite as possible, I stood firm that she was still going to have to move. She leaned over and pulled her stakes. Bruce watched the whole thing from the truck, elbow out the window.

"Nice," he said, when I hopped back in. "I thought a college boy like you would cave at the waterworks."

It was around this time, with begrudging approval, that he added yet another nickname to the growing list. He was telling me I did a good job at some particular task and casually said, "Yeah, but you'll be a one-season wonder." The park sees scores of rangers who show up, appear to love the work, and then find something else to do the following summer.

All the little things I did right seemed to add up in that balding cranium of his, however. Maybe I wasn't so bad, though he still didn't get me.

"What's underground music?" he asked me one day. "Underground. By that you mean crap, right? That no one else likes." If a band didn't have widespread appeal, he argued, there was a reason. He felt the same about my undying love of Liverpool Football Club. "Football? That's not football. No one likes soccer, certainly not any red-blooded American male."

But I was growing on him.

One morning, Bruce stepped into the office and presented me with a routed sign, brown with white lettering spelling out "Andrew Vietze." I figured it meant I'd arrived as a ranger. It was for the front wall of the station, underneath the signs that read "Rangers:" and "Bruce White." Tradition at Baxter Park held that stations bore the names of those on duty. I thought it meant he finally approved.

Not so much, I found out later. He had a whole bunch of signs with similar names, the rangers who'd come before, that he nailed up chronologically on his "Wall of Shame." I was just another in a long list.

CHAPTER 8

EVEN THOUGH THE SUMMER OF 2020 HAS BARELY BEGUN, EVERYTHING is already withering from lack of rain. The roadsides are brown. The grass is tawny. Leaves droop on the trees, and some have already dropped to the ground. Fire danger remains high across the state, and Bruce told his staff to put our firefighting gear on the backs of our trucks, just to be prudent.

I get two backpack pumps and use some webbing to lash them to the cab. Then I find a trash can with a cover. This will keep the pump out of the weather. With its Honda four-stroke engine, this little water thrower is astonishingly powerful, shooting about 100 gallons a minute through an inch-and-a-half hose, at about 60 pounds per square inch. It's strong enough to push water 100 feet or more up a steep incline and will go for hours or even days if it's well maintained.

Every spring I drag the pump to Daicey's shore to charge the water line to my camp, filling the black plastic hose with enough H_2O to create the draw from the pond that powers my gravity-powered shower. This not only simplifies the priming process but also keeps me practiced on pump operation and ensures our pump is ready for action.

After the Honda goes a shovel and a Pulaski. Named for Edward Pulaski, an assistant ranger with the U.S. Forest Service, this tool looks like an ax with a grub hoe on the back, and it's used to dig fire lines—removing everything burnable in front of a fire, down to the mineral layer—among many other outdoor tasks. Pulaski made his name during the Great Fire of 1910, also known as the Big Burn, saving most of his crew from the conflagration that raged across parts of the western United States.

A native of Idaho, Pulaski didn't start working as a ranger until the age of 40, having spent his early life blacksmithing, farming, and building. He became one of a generation of "ranger-inventors" who used their experience, ingenuity, and mechanical aptitude to customize tools for the backcountry. Pulaski took a combination shovel, ax, and hoe created by another ranger, removed the shovel head, and made improvements to invent the simple firefighting implement that would bear his name. He tinkered until he was satisfied, and the resulting tool became so popular in the Rockies that it went into commercial manufacturing. Today, it's a staple of wildland firefighting. Step into a ranger station anywhere in the country, and you'll likely find a Pulaski in the corner.

We have our own breed of ranger-tinkerers at Baxter. This inventiveness comes with the territory and the trade—because of the remoteness of the park, it's often hard to get supplies when we need them. In that way, it's similar to living on an island. If we need a tool or a piece of hardware, we might have to wait weeks to get it. So we often find it easier to come up with our own creations to solve very specific problems rather than try to find commercial ones that only somewhat fit our needs. When the park couldn't find a wood splitter rugged enough for the amount of wood we process—at least not at the price administrators wanted to pay—Ranger Barry MacArthur welded a frame together from old girders and hooked up some hydraulics to an engine, creating a Frankensplitter that we all used for decades.

We've also created our own backpack litter carry rig for transporting patients and retrofitted a mobile firefighting tank to supply water to ranger housing during dry summers. Lester Kenway, who ran the Baxter Park trail crew a few years before I arrived, has become something of a living legend in backcountry recreation areas across the country. Kenway won several national awards for innovation in trail work, and some called his Griphoist, a rig that allows crews to pluck rocks from streambeds hundreds of feet below without disturbing the surroundings, nothing short of revolutionary.

Bruce uses egg beaters with his 20-volt cordless drill when he makes his famous carrot cake for ranger get-togethers and once even hooked up a washing machine at Katahdin Stream, using runoff from the mountain to clean his uniforms. (No soap ever got back into the waterway.) He, Charity, and I built bracing for kayak seats when the plastic braces on several in our fleet broke. Bruce and I came to the idea separately at the same time; his design was better than mine, and we were able to put a handful of boats back in the water rather than buy new.

I put a gas can and water pump toolbox onto the truck and think to myself that this pump has fought one blaze already this spring. Lowering the pump into the trash can reminds me how heavy these vital engines are. I've only had to haul one of these to a fire, and I only carried it a short way.

––––––––––

The summer of 2007 was a dry one, not unlike the first few months of this year. The National Weather Service reported that September of that year, my fifth in the park, "would be remembered for its warmth and extended period of dry weather." Almost half the country experienced a moderate to severe drought, and the woods around Katahdin were no exception, seeing about 10 percent of the normal amount of precipitation.

In early October, one of the local flying services called in a smoke sighting in Baxter Park. This set radios abuzz across the park, and I listened keenly to the one in the back pocket of my tactical pants as I went about my chores. Hikers on the mountain reported that they, too, saw a column of smoke, and the Maine Forest Service eventually came to check, confirming a blaze in the Windy Pitch area.

When this came across the radio it really got my attention. Windy Pitch was in my neighborhood. I radioed Bob Howes, one of the supervisory rangers, and suggested I jog down the trail to see what I could see.

"Why don't you hold off on that, Andy," came the reply.

When you are a ranger and you know there's action out there, it can be difficult to think about anything but that action. At least for this ranger. I returned to raking but kept pausing to listen to my radio. Eventually, I gave up and went into the office to better hear all the traffic on the base radio. When talk of "putting a crew together" came across the air, I made for my truck and drove over to Kidney Pond, uninvited.

Bob was leaning on the hood of a truck, looking at the big DeLorme map of Baxter Park and trying to pinpoint the location of the conflagration from the coordinates the Forest Service radioed in when I got there. A helicopter wheeled over the campground, roaring along low. Other rangers arrived in trucks, everyone gathering gear, backpack pumps, Pulaskis, rakes, shovels, chain saws, helmets, and hundreds of feet of hose. It began to look like the staging area for a military operation. Campers gathered, watching excitedly. I assembled a pack and began hauling hand tools down to the canoe landing.

As the ranking ranger on scene, Bob gave us our orders. It was too late in the day to try and put the fire out. We were to hump gear in, determine the size of the fire, flag an access trail, and cut a landing zone for the Forest Service. The seven-person team was composed of Bruce, supervisory ranger Rob Tice, and me; trail crew supervisor Paul Sannicandro, crew leader Michael Garrigan; and two of Garrigan's charges, Summer and Blake, who had already climbed the mountain that day to do trail work on high.

Reaching the fire was part of the challenge: we had to paddle across 96-acre Kidney Pond, beach the canoes at Lily Pond Landing, hike with all the gear down to Lily Pad Pond, canoe to the far end of that small basin, and finally bushwhack on foot through the thick woods above Windy Pitch. As we did so, we took in a landscape that already looked on fire, covered in autumnal reds and oranges and yellows. We didn't tarry to enjoy it. Even so, by the time we reached the far shore of Lily Pad, a meandering pond underneath a panorama of Katahdin, it was after 5 P.M. From there, it would be a carry.

We each took a load and began to thread single file down the trail to Windy Pitch—a tiny basin ringed by small hills—our helmets and chain saw chaps and water bottles banging on our backs, like the noisiest patrol of combat grunts ever. The path paralleled wide Nesowadnehunk Stream and the Appalachian Trail on the far side of it before breaking away for the final half-mile to Windy Pitch. As I hiked, I wondered how big the blaze would be, imagining a towering wall, crowning the treetops.

The small pool at Windy Pitch would provide the water we needed to control whatever conflagration we found. The park has a canoe on this tiny waterbody, but at 8 acres, Windy Pitch is hardly big enough to paddle. You pushed off on one side and reached the other in what seemed like seconds. I hoped we weren't going to suck it dry.

Small foothills climb up over the pond, and it was on one of these that the fire was located. We started up one, Bruce like a bloodhound with a GPS in one hand and a compass in the other. The climb was quite a bushwhack, leaving us tripping over underbrush and getting gear tangled in tree branches. About halfway up we began to smell smoke.

"It's about three-tenths of a mile from here," Bruce told us as we struggled through the thicket. It took us another half hour to crest the hill and, in the gathering dusk, get our first glimpse: smoke and lots of it. I thought, *We're never going to be able to outrun an out-of-control wall of fire up here.* The area was simply too densely forested.

The smoke emanated from a mound of spruce trees, the largest probably 18 inches in diameter, all in a jumble one on top of the next, blackened and charred on the underside. Beneath, in a sinkhole of moss, the blaze shot flames up 3 feet high at their tallest. The burn was strong, encompassing an area about as large as a good-sized house, and it showed no sign of going out. All around this little hilltop bog was a forest of dry leaves, needles, and dead conifers. If we didn't stop the fire here, we'd be fighting to keep it from consuming the cabins at Kidney.

Bruce started his saw, and he and Blake and I started cutting a perimeter around the fire, pulling any fuel we could away from the embers. From the hill we could see a clearing on the side opposite the pond. It looked like the best place around, really the only place, to land a helo. The sun was yawning its last rays, so Rob told us to take the saw down and join Paul and Mike, who had begun widening the little meadow.

"Cutting the LZ is the priority now," he said.

We put up a few glow sticks in the trees to mark the gear and the trail, and then we switched on our headlamps, making our way down to the clearing. Though boggy, the ground seemed firm enough to support a helicopter, and we felled all the small trees that we found. After an hour or so, we pushed out from the center, cutting and throwing until Rob said he thought it was a big enough space to accommodate a chopper.

We lost the light and couldn't saw safely, so Bob told us to turn for Kidney. We followed a trail that Rob had flagged, climbing over, around, and through a forest of dense conifers in the dark, which filled our underpants with pine needles. It was slow going. Bob asked for three volunteers to join the Maine Forest Service rangers and their team of wildland firefighting specialists, the Hot Shots, the next day. I raised my hand, despite knowing full well it would be long hours of hauling and lifting, hot and wet. Like wilderness rescue, firefighting is more grime than glamour. By the time we reached Kidney, paddling in under cover of darkness, it was well past quitting time and I had several minor bleeds.

The whole group squeezed elbow to elbow into the Kidney Pond Ranger Station, where we were fed a three-course dinner: chips, sandwich, cookies. I learned from my boss, Jodi Browning, that the Maine Forest Service actually needed only two rangers, and I made the cut. Not only that, Rob Tice and I would be flying in the next morning with gear and the Houlton Hot Shot crew.

Of course, I could hardly sleep.

First thing the next day, Rob and I rallied with Forest Service ranger Will Barnum at Slaughter Pit, one of the few LZs in the park. The Hot Shots were delayed, so we'd come back for them. Soon the quiet was broken by the rhythmic pulsation of an incoming helicopter, and we watched an army-green Huey appear over the trees of the pit and come to rest in the dirt. Maine Forest Service pilot John Knight touched down and we climbed aboard, heads low to avoid decapitation. We strapped in, lifted off, banked to the southeast, and enjoyed the kind of foliage show that people usually pay for. It was only a minute or so to the fire, and John began to circle above. The hole in the bog we cut the previous night didn't look as big from the air as it did by the light of headlamps. John decided it was too small for the windy conditions. That sucked because it meant all the gear would need to be hand-carried overland, and we hadn't even seen our crew yet.

Our two Forest Service brothers decided to use a little neck on Lily Pad Pond to offload supplies—we scared both a person fishing and a moose as we lowered down to test the spot—so that most of the gear not already on-site would only have to be lugged a mile. I was glad I had all those Hot Shots to help.

Only we didn't. The crew we were expecting was dispatched to another fire in Aroostook County, and only four were joining our fight. We were faced with more work and fewer people to do it, but it's hard to get discouraged flying the friendly skies of Baxter Park in a Huey, even if it rocks and groans like an antique bus, with just a thin bit of metal between passengers and the ground. I couldn't imagine taking heavy fire in one of these. I was glad the fisherman and the moose didn't get hostile.

The chief had originally decided not to use campground rangers to fight this blaze, simply because of operational needs. Someone had to keep the place running, clean sites, check in visitors, and be available to respond to other emergencies. But the situation forced his hand, and he allocated more park personnel to help.

Bruce and I, along with Student Conservation Association intern Mei-Ling Chung, led a team of four Hot Shots down the Appalachian Trail, crossing the old Toll Dam bridge and climbing the riverbank to Windy Pitch Trail. This required balancing on a decrepit old log across raging Nesowadnehunk Stream and threading through walls of alders, but it freed up the canoes at Kidney Pond for camper use. From there, we met Rob and Will at Lily Pad, who helped haul gear.

By lunchtime, we'd only made it as far as Big Niagara Falls, having explored a couple of other water source options, cutting through country as dense as I'd ever encountered. But we ultimately concluded that Windy Pitch was the way to go. Reaching the pond required more than a mile of hose, and with our small crew hauling big, square, canvas backpacks full of 300 or 400 feet, each weighing 40 or 50 pounds, it took until about four in the afternoon to make all the connections and start shooting water.

As the Hot Shots doused the flames, Bruce and I dug with rakes and Pulaskis to ensure that the water reached embers burrowed deep in the bog. While we worked, I asked Will if he thought, as we did, that this must have been the result of a lightning strike. He figured that a bolt had probably hit a couple of weeks ago and sparked a small blaze, which grew as the bog dried from lack of rain.

(I couldn't help thinking about the lightning strike fatality Bruce and I had responded to a little more than a month before and cursed Thor and his bolts. It was the darkest moment of my Baxter Park career. I'll never shake the sound of the wail the victim's mother made that day.)

As we dug, and the Hot Shots poured, Will measured the perimeter of the blaze—it entered the Maine Forest Service annals as the .07-acre Windy Pitch Fire. We worked another couple of hours, turning over soil and raining water on the bog, before Will called us off. A Hot Shot crew returned the next day to supersaturate the ground and perform the never fun task of mop-up.

I lucked out of that duty. It was back to toilets for me, thankfully. I'd rather spend twenty minutes scrubbing hoppers than a whole day lugging wet hose.

My good fortune held. Two days later, Bruce and I were sent by our boss, Jodi, to check on the fire. We hiked in, enjoying the fall foliage and the opportunity to get back into the woods, while everyone else was dealing with leaf peepers. The moss-covered knoll was a big puddle of wet black guck, with hoses still snaking down the hill. The Forest Service decided to leave everything in place in case of any flare-ups. As we walked around the site, Bruce and I marveled that the fire had stayed within the bounds of the bog despite all the crispy leaves, dried-out needles, and dehydrated spruce trees available to it. Everything was parched for miles and miles and miles around.

Despite the relative tameness of the fire itself, it was an exciting few days—paddling Kidney and Lily Pad ponds in the dark, wheeling over the park in a Huey, firing up the hoses. And while I was glad for the excitement, I was also relieved we caught the blaze early, before it had a chance to puff out its chest and become a genuine conflagration.

I missed out on most of the other firefighting action during my decades with the park. Power lines started a blaze just a day before I was to return to duty one year, and a small fire on Togue Pond needed only a handful of rangers to combat. I was on duty that date, and, again, itching to get there, but I was not sent and couldn't think of an excuse to drive all the way to Togue. The only other fire I fought was a tiny AT campfire left behind by some illegal campers.

One near opportunity came on a day in 2017 when a fuel shed burned at the Abol Bridge Store on the park's perimeter, down near the Penobscot River. I happened to be in the south end and was deployed, driving the "water buffalo," a 500-gallon portable tank and pump on a trailer, across the old, pothole-ridden State Road to the scene. It was the bumpiest, most brutal ride I can remember, the truck and the tank whiplashing from crater to crater. By the time I reached the fire it was almost out, with Millinocket Fire Department and the Maine Forest Service already in place. Bruce arrived with the huge old fire truck that the Forest Service loans the park every summer, and we were both told *thanks, but we got it.*

The drive itself was the adventure that day, and as I was banging along on the way back to the park, I considered what might have happened if that fire was not controlled quickly. The whole southeast corner of Baxter Park sits out the back door of Abol Bridge, including our snow-sled sheds, a series of other bridges, and the park housing at Abol Field. A slow response, a stiff wind, and some hillsides filled with dead wood could have made for disaster.

At the park we prepare as best we can for fire. We do annual spring training. We limit fires in the backcountry, and frontcountry rangers like

Charity and I go site to site each year to make sure our firepits are free of vegetation and other combustibles. We have caches of firefighting tools at each duty station, including pumps, Pulaskis, and several hundred feet of hose.

Attitudes toward wildland fire response have changed dramatically across the nation in the past half century. Up until the 1960s, the general consensus at the U.S. Forest Service and other forest management agencies was that when Hephaestus walked in the wildlands, firefighters should do battle. Suppress, suppress, suppress. But wilderness biologists began to argue that fire is a natural part of forest ecology, and some flora suffer for the lack of it.

Conflagrations return essential nutrients to the soil faster than decomposition, and they open up space in the canopy of the woods to allow light in. At Baxter Park, for example, we know that the blueberry barrens love to burn and that moose, the park's most popular residents, like nothing better than to munch the new growth that appears shortly after an area is seared by flame. (It seems as if fire knows this—all the blazes I can think of, from the big one in 1977 to the one this spring along the Penobscot, burned where we have big clusters of blueberry plants.)

The park has responded with a fire plan based on causation. We suppress every human-lit fire. When nature sparks a blaze, we assess it based upon the impact it will have on our neighbors, our facilities, and other resources and respond accordingly.

As a kid who grew up hankering to pull on turnout gear and a helmet, I have conflicting emotions when it comes to fires like these. I don't want the park to burn, but I'd like to help put it out if it does.

CHAPTER 9

"WE DIDN'T EXPECT TO SEE YOU HERE," SAYS A PLEASANT, MIDDLE-AGED redhead with a big smile.

Standing on the porch of the ranger station, talking to me through the window, she introduces her balding husband and tells me they're up from Massachusetts.

"Why not?" I ask.

"When we checked in there was no ranger. They told us at the gate there would be no ranger when we arrived."

"Ah," I say. "My partner and I have been out the past couple of weeks, and we've had a lot of different rangers filling in." Charity was sick. I'd used some vacation time.

"Anyway, we were saying," the woman points to her husband, "we didn't see why there needed to be a ranger anyway. What is there even for a ranger to do here?"

"Well," I explain, "we check people in. We rescue people. We rent canoes. We maintain all of these century-old cabins. We cut the firewood. We put out fires. We clean the toilets—"

"Oh," she says, cutting me off. She turns to her husband: "I guess we do need rangers."

———

Everyone has their own ideas about park rangers, and there seems to be a lot of goodwill in the American psyche for those who wear the badge, at least from those who aren't trying to get away with something. A few, however, consider us "pine pigs"—cops with forest-green uniforms. These might include the small percentage of AT thru-hikers who think it's a grotesque affront that we ask for $10 a night at the Birches. Having bivvied wherever they felt like putting down their sleeping bag for hundreds of miles, some consider this fee too much. They're happy to come in without the reservations that all the other campers in Baxter Park must make, use the clean outhouses, and enjoy the free use of day packs so they don't have to hump their big rucks up the mountain. They'll gladly take our help connecting them with whomever might be picking them up, ask us to call a shuttle for them, or accept a ride in the back of a park truck. But don't expect them to *pay* for any of this.

Then there are those visitors for whom even the most basic of rules—carry out your trash, don't bathe in the water source, leave the dog at home, bring only as many people as your site allows—are a little too onerous. Years ago, I was the recipient of a nasty-gram from a couple who thought that way. My supervisor was shocked because I'd never had people complain about my behavior as a ranger, and she wanted my version of the story. In a scathing note, a woman from Hampden wrote that she and her husband "are not 'wild' or 'law-breaking looking people.'" I had cautioned them about trolling on the pond, after observing her husband with 20 feet of line in the water as she paddled the canoe around. I also asked her parents to move their car after they drove past the 4-foot sign that reads "Driving Beyond This Point Is for Daicey Pond Campers Only" and parked in a disability spot, despite the fact that they were not Daicey Pond campers and had no disability card.

I was pleased to have the opportunity to respond to the letter. I didn't get into park ranger work out of any sort of desire to be a lawman, but I'm a true believer in Percival Baxter's mission, and I'll point out infractions when I see them. This particular group seemed slightly paranoid from the moment I pulled out my little notebook to check them in, visiting their site because they didn't check in at the ranger station. They eyed me as if to say, *Why's he pulling out his book and writing us up?* It's routine at check-in to look at a group's reservation and to write down the name and number in the party. I smiled and told jokes. They weren't having any of it. Luckily, I had a ranger with me during the trolling incident who backed me up, and other rangers dealt with this group during the rest of their stay.

These incidents prompted the young woman to tell me that she didn't appreciate me talking to them like that because they "have master's degrees" and that "the kind of people who break the rules are not the kind of people who come to Baxter State Park." I've heard this line from a lot of visitors.

I wish it were true.

When my family camped at Baxter Park, my parents always stressed that this place, quite aside from being magic, was a gift, and we had an almost reverential attitude toward the park. Many others think of it in the same way.

But thousands don't. We've had people drive stolen cars into the park, bring firearms into their cabins, kick in outhouse walls, carve up cabins, launch motorboats on Daicey Pond, fly prohibited drones, smash the thwarts of canoes to unlock them and use them illegally, and pack twenty people into a cabin that fits six. Drunks have broken into my cabin. I've been threatened, and many of my fellow rangers have as well. And litter . . . oh, the litter. I've fished a lot of trash out of outhouses and on most days my pockets are filled with bread ties and napkins, granola bar wrappers and beer caps. I've personally seen countless speeders, and at least four or five times a day I have to ask people who elect to ignore the signage, like the nasty-gram author's parents, to move their car down to the day-use lot.

Some of the people responsible for these acts might even have master's degrees.

———————

Besides these folks, though, most people really do seem to appreciate rangers. They see us as walking Americana. Rugged individualists. The personification of the wilderness. We hold a vaunted place in popular culture, known as naturalists, foresters, firefighters, and rescuers. I can't count the number of times people have told me they wish they had my job (until they see me cleaning an outhouse).

It's amusing, though, how little they know about what we do. Even many of our regulars are uncertain what exactly happens in that mysterious office and why I'm usually not in there. Some think we are *federales*, employees of the National Park Service. Despite the name Baxter *State* Park, these folks like to ask what other national parks I've been stationed at.

"Have you ever worked at Acadia?" they ask. "Grand Canyon? Denali?"

I've never worked for the NPS, and I can't transfer to Yellowstone or Big Bend. I would have to apply for a job in the National Park Service and start at the bottom like anyone else. My background would likely make me a good candidate—I'm a Registered Maine Guide with more than 15 years of professional experience as a park ranger—but I work for Baxter.

I can't even transfer within Maine's state park system, because Baxter State Park is, again, despite the name, not actually a state park. Along with the Allagash Wilderness Waterway, it sits outside the Bureau of Parks and Lands' 48-site state-park system. It is in no way related to Sebago Lake or Camden Hills or Bradbury Mountain or Reid or any other state park. It takes no outside monies and is a self-sustaining, self-governed, independent entity that happens to belong to the people of Maine.

Neither am I a *forest* ranger in the employ of the Maine Forest Service or the U.S. Forest Service. These individuals fight wildfires and enforce harvesting laws, among other duties. They train at the Maine Criminal Justice Academy, just like state troopers and game wardens. I have a soft spot for our region's forest rangers because they help with rescues, often dropping from the sky to airlift our patients so we don't have to haul them down the mountain. Nothing beats hearing the distant pitter-patter of an inbound helicopter when you're on a mission.

I've been asked on numerous occasions whether I've ever been on *North Woods Law*, the popular Animal Planet show about the adventures of Maine's warden service. While we share a boss with these officers and take on some similar tasks, we are not the same. Wardens are woods cops who enforce hunting and fishing regulations. They also train at the Maine Criminal Justice Academy, earning full commissions, like state troopers and local police officers. They patrol vast districts in the woods, and even in Portland, and are responsible for statewide search-and-rescue operations.

I'm not a fisheries biologist, either. Or a forester, another assumption people make.

I'm just a frontcountry Baxter Park ranger. And I'm happy with my lot.

Because they equate us with National Park Service staff, many park visitors expect to find us seated at our desks, no matter the time of day, like interpretive rangers at national parks. Unlike those rangers, however, we actually *range*. Meaning we move about.

My duty station might be next to a picturesque pond on the southwest side of the park, but my work on any given day could take me from south of the gate to Matagamon Lake, an hour and a half to the north, and anywhere in between. "Other duties as assigned," as the park puts it. I spend a lot of time helping out at neighboring Kidney Pond and Katahdin Stream campgrounds, and their rangers can regularly be found at Daicey Pond when I need an extra set of hands. I am sent on rescues or firefighting missions or tree-cutting details wherever they might happen in the park.

Campers unfamiliar with the ways of Baxter Park often look at me like I've been shirking duty when I return to the station from one of these projects afield. But they wouldn't be happy if the outhouses were filthy, there was no wood for their cabins, the buildings were falling down around them, or the place was on fire.

———

One of the aspects of my job that I love most is that I get to clean toilets. "Where else can you play six holes every morning?" I tell campers, who grimace when I'm up to the elbows in a toilet riser. (All credit to retired ranger Mark Varney, former emperor of Varneyville, a.k.a. Nesowadnehunk Campground, from whom I stole that line.)

"Fecal Strike Force, Special Forces, Dark Ops," I'll tell others.

"That must be the worst part of your job," campers will often say. And I think to myself, *no, that would be fetching a body bag,* but I just smile. Or reply that "cleaning toilets is the ranger's most brave and noble task."

Do I really enjoy being a defecation commando? Not so much, especially not after chili night or late in the season when the seats get cold and people hunch over the hole and miss.

But scrubbing the Daicey bogs allows me to do all the things that I truly love.

Allow me to explain.

At a national park, janitors tend to the facilities, and that's all they do. The NPS has contracted custodians whose only role is to make sure the urinals are clean. They don't fight fires. They don't go on rescues. They don't get to play with helicopters. They scrub one set of johns and drive on to find the next one.

The NPS specialized its workforce decades ago. At Acadia, law enforcement rangers patrol in vehicles that look like cop cruisers, only with more green. Interpretive rangers point out the sights and answer questions. Maintenance staff work on infrastructure. Trail crews handle all the trail work. Specialized teams fight fires and deploy on searches and rescues.

At Baxter Park we get to do it all, and the variety makes the job for me. I wouldn't want to sit in the ranger station at Daicey all day long and simply greet visitors, explaining where they can find moose. ("Canada," I usually tell those who ask.) The four log walls would get close pretty quickly. I like to range. I need to range.

Here, I roof cabins, enforce the rules, brush out trails, put up signage, fight fires, respond to vehicle accidents, spend the night searching for lost parties on the mountain, work with helicopters, and pluck AT hikers out of the stream.

If the park were a hotel, I'd be the clerk who cheerfully checks you in, giving you all the information you need to enjoy your stay. But I'd also be the concierge who briefs you on where to find all the sites you want to see on your visit. And the physical plant maintenance person who makes sure everything works properly. And the custodian who cleans your room.

And the security guy who patrols the facility, ensuring everyone is safe and nothing illegal goes on. I'd be the first responder who patches you up when you fall on the stairs . . . or worse. The lifeguard who watches over the pool. The firefighter who puts out the blaze when someone drops a cigarette. The arborist who cuts trees bent over in a storm, the manager of the little shop with the maps and books, the landscaper who mows the lawn and works on the pathways, the chimney sweep who climbs onto the roof, the naturalist who tells you what kind of bird that is, the road worker who fills potholes out front, the roadside service driver who gives you a jump or changes your tire, and the woodcutter who cuts, splits, and stacks cords of firewood to keep you warm.

Being a ranger, as former Maine attorney general Steve Rowe once said to me, means being good at both hard and soft skills. And a lot of each.

When I sign on in the morning with "Daicey Pond is 10-8," I don't know what the day will bring. I have a pretty good idea—most days are, broadly, cleaning in the morning, maintenance in the afternoon, check-ins and camper orientation at night. But none of it is certain. I could be called away for something else at any minute.

And I'm thankful for that.

———————

"Do you have an air compressor? We have a flat."

I recognize the young woman from Cabin 4, up for a weekend with a bunch of friends, probably just out of college. They're heading out. Or were, until they found a flat on the right rear of their Subaru Forester.

I tangled with some members of her party just a few minutes ago, a couple of 20-something guys bent on proving they're bad boys. One of them lifted the BSP Vehicles Only sign by the woodshed and backed his van across the lawn and all the way up to his site.

All of our sites are walk-in at Daicey, and apparently this guy had a problem with that. He had a problem with me, too, when I told him to move the vehicle, giving me a Manson stare until he realized I wasn't going to back down. Eventually, he started up his Ford Transit and growled his way down into the lot while I replaced the sign. When he walked back by, I said, "Heed the signage, will ya?"

He nodded.

Now they needed me. I trotted down to my personal vehicle and grabbed my air compressor. It seems we change or pump at least one tire per shift. I give the kids my compressor, and as its dull roar echoes across the amphitheater that is the pond, the young woman walks over to me.

"I would love to work here," she says between takes on her vape pen.

"It's a pretty great gig," I say.

"What kind of training do you have to have to get a job here?"

I get this question all the time, especially after people learn that my previous job was as a magazine writer. I explain that we do a lot of on-the-job training and that the park doesn't necessarily require that people have degrees in any particular field. Or even degrees at all.

Our instructional regimen has grown steadily since I began at the park. We still require chain saw training, a one- or two-day program that begins with saw basics and safety, proceeds through cutting cookies and notches, and ends with felling, using the bore-cut method. I've been through it three or four times now, under different auspices: ATC, MEMIC, and Game of Logging.

Some of the new rangers struggle with saw use, and we've had a few conscientious objectors in recent years who refuse to cut down live trees. (One of this year's sensitive probies told his supervisor that sawing a healthy tree hurt his soul. "I'll pray for your soul," said the boss. "You cut the tree.") We use saws a fair amount in the field, cutting blowdowns, clearing roads and campgrounds, eliminating hazards, and readying firewood.

Every couple of years we also go through an introduction to firefighting taught by our brothers and sisters at the Maine Forest Service, who combat blazes as their primary occupation. We all look forward to these days, not for learning how to work pumps and cut fire lines, but because they often include a ride over the park in one of the Forest Service's helicopters. Some of us have continued our firefighting education by attending the more advanced Wildland Firefighter 1 course that the Forest Service offers occasionally. Because it was scheduled in the off-season, I missed half of this class, but I was able to get the same instruction through FEMA. Then I followed it up with a second training in the spring.

Two senior rangers host Baxter Park's own Introduction to Search and Rescue, another class that I've been through several times. (So many times that on multiple occasions our meetings had to be postponed due to an actual lost person or rescue.) In this one-day affair, newbies walk through GPS use, patient transport, grid searches, and the ins and outs of SAR in the park, usually leavened with a lot of first-person tales. In recent years, many of us have also taken Maine Association for Search and Rescue's much more thorough basic course.

And everyone must become certified in wilderness medicine to at least the wilderness first-aid level. I've taken this class through SOLO, NOLS, and Wilderness Medical Associates more times than I can count, and many of the protocols have changed. We never used to be allowed to apply tourniquets to a major bleed, for example. Thanks to new data from the battlefields of Iraq and Afghanistan, however, this has become common practice. We used to stick each other with syringes in the event we had to inject epinephrine into a patient suffering from anaphylaxis. Now we shoot up oranges or bundles of gauze instead of our fellow rangers. And don't get me started on CPR, the best practices of which change almost annually.

For years, I harangued my supervisor, telling her that I'd never been anywhere where learning didn't progress, where you take the same class over and over. The point finally got through to one of our new chief rangers, who began to offer Wilderness *Advanced* First Aid and eventually Wilderness First Responder. Now many of us have the latter qualification, which allows us to engage in some field protocols that historically superseded what even street EMTs could do. This is because theoretically, and often in practice, we treat patients deep in the back-country where advanced life support, or ALS, is often hours and hours away. In the park, you can't simply bundle an injured individual into an ambulance and be in a state-of-the-art hospital in minutes. Litter carries can take hours or days, and overnighting on the slopes of Katahdin with a patient is not uncommon.

Most years we attend helicopter training, often with both the Maine Forest Service and the Maine National Guard's 101st out of Bangor. Sometimes these sessions are in the field, occasionally at the airport in Millinocket. The Forest Service began a short-haul program several years back, and the training fills us in on our role in the process so we can help their crews. This includes picking locations for extraction, signaling to the helicopter, and using radio comms. Short hauls involve "human external cargo"; in other words, a crew member and the patient dangle below the helicopter for the entire ride at the end of a 150-foot line. Most of the crew have less medical training than we do, simply serving to package and guide the patient in a transport-harness called a "Screamer Suit." At short-haul trainings we all jockey to be the patient, wanting to see the park from the sky, but it's a ride only a handful have taken and I've never been fortunate enough.

The Maine National Guard drops medics down lines as well, but the medic disconnects and readies the patient to be hoisted into the aircraft via an external winch. In helo sessions with the Guard, they explain general protocols and how best to help them from the ground, as well as "hot loading," which is running a stretcher to the aircraft while it's touched down and its rotors are revolving.

Those classes—first aid, SAR, firefighting, chain saw, and helo—constitute our basic training, and we all go through them at least every few years. While I've been at the park, these courses have been augmented by a host of others. I've completed several levels of incident command training, learning how to run a rescue. I've done ride-alongs with the year-round staff to better understand their jobs.

I've frozen in a pond during a flatwater rescue class, getting schooled on how to deal with capsized canoes and haul people over the gunwales. I've sat through a Fourth Amendment seminar, exploring my rights when it comes to search and seizure. (The instructor compared us to Batman because many of us are uncommissioned but still carry out the will of the state.)

I attended a death investigation workshop the year after we had four fatalities in the park. In that gruesome, illustrated lecture, the state's coroner taught us what to look for if we come across a fatality, how to not disturb a scene, how to secure fragile evidence, and how to identify all types of bodily bloat and decay. She did this with a big smile on her face, constantly cracking jokes, while many rangers peeked at the screen through their fingers.

We've learned how to de-escalate tense situations in Verbal Judo class. We've attended sessions on native Penobscot culture, because Katahdin, of course, is a sacred place to these indigenous peoples. And we've sat through workshops on how to help people suffering from mental distress, scheduled in the aftermath of a few ugly "10-44" situations. In one, a kid from Millinocket stole a car, drove into the park, and tried to kill himself by repeatedly bashing his head on a rock before driving around the south end, bleeding heavily from his cranium, and asking people if they had a gun. My partner Charity ultimately met him on the road and talked quietly to him until help could arrive to cuff him and get him the care he needed.

An AT thru-hiker with the trail name "Socket," out of his mind on some sort of rocket fuel, freaked out other climbers on Hunt Trail with his ranting and erratic behavior. He spent the night on the mountain and must have sweated the stuff out through his pores because when another ranger and I found him the next morning, he was gentle as a kitten, telling us all about his dog, Winston, a pup that hiked all the way from Georgia with him and was at Abol Bridge with a trail buddy, "playing poker." Winston would enter park lore for his skills at cards.

A transient woman entered and exited the park down by Abol Beach, her mind cracked by substances. Another guy drove around in a car packed to the roof with junk, so out of his head on something that he couldn't comprehend our camping-in-a-designated-site-only policy. We had so many of these lost souls that season—drug addled, intent on self-harm, or simply with a mental map lacking the typical trails—that I complained to a state trooper buddy about the preponderance of 10-44s.

"Don't even start," he said to me. "That's our primary customer."

———————

The next season, just a few weeks after going through the National Alliance on Mental Illness's Mental Health First Aid training, I put to use what I learned when a severely dehydrated, linebacker-size guy in his 20s, covered in white nationalist tats, dropped right on the doorstep of my office in the late afternoon and refused to move. Like many southbound thru-hikers, he intended to trek the 6 miles out of the park and put up a tent at Daicey Pond if he couldn't make it. I told him we had cabins only and all were currently booked.

"Can't I just put up a tent?"

"We don't have tent sites," I explained.

"Well, I'm not going anywhere."

He told me he had climbed the mountain on the previous day in the suffocating humidity and high-80s heat and just barely made it, coming down in the dark. He'd spent the last eight hours stumbling his way along the AT 2.5 miles from Katahdin Stream.

"I passed out a lot," he told me. "I crawled some, too."

I got him some water, sat him in the shade, put a cool towel on his forehead, and started to perform a patient assessment. He was big enough that I hoped he'd comply with my questions, which were the standard things: allergies, last food and drink, and whether or not he took any medication.

"I was on medication back home, but I didn't want to carry it. Figured I couldn't get it refilled anyway."

"What kind of meds?"

"Stuff for my head. I'm not supposed to be around other people," he said. "My wife has a restraining order. That's why I'm out here. The judge thought it would be a good idea."

His problem list also included black urine and severe back pain, which I took to be his kidneys.

I radioed this to the chief.

"Will he get into an ambulance?"

My huge patient nodded.

This seemed to be in the best interest of both of us. He could be rehydrated and checked for rhabdomyolysis, and he could talk to a doc because he was off his meds (this was a point made over and over in Mental Health First Aid); I could keep the park safe from a giant who's not supposed to be around other people.

The chief and I decided to put him comfortably in the back of a truck and meet the ambulance. Ranger Nick Macpherson from Katahdin Stream arrived, and we walked the fellow down the hill to Nick's truck.

"Figured you could use some backup," Nick said. A young dude from southern Maine, Nick had started on the trail crew and spent a season at Roaring Brook before Bruce recruited him for Katahdin Stream. We'd performed a number of late-night rescues on the Abol Trail together. "When I heard you say 'big guy off his meds' . . . "

"Thanks, man."

He switched on the emergency lights, and we zipped down to meet the ambulance at the entrance to Katahdin Stream. I'd be away from my campground a while, and upon my return would probably get raised eyebrows from campers who expected me to be at my desk, but I figured everyone would agree it was for the best.

Above: Daicey Pond offers one of the finest views of Katahdin anywhere. *Photo by Jennifer Smith Mayo.*

Below: My camp sits underneath a fantastic view of Doubletop Mountain, about 100 yards from the Appalachian Trail. *Photo by Lisa Mossel Vietze.*

Above: The ranger station at Daicey Pond. I like to joke that my name's on a building. *Photo by the author.*

Above: Katahdin Stream Campground, one of the major trailheads and an Appalachian Trail hub, was my first duty station. *Photo by Fredlyfish4, Creative Commons on Wikimedia.*

Right: Baxter State Park unit 6-13 on the job. *Photo by Lisa Mossel Vietze.*

Next pages: The Knife Edge is a classic granite arête. We typically perform several rescues a year on its long spine. *Photo by Fredlyfish4, Creative Commons on Wikimedia.*

Above: Ranger Justine Rumaker, former ranger Ryleigh Davis, me, and my son Gus working on the bridge at Katahdin Stream Falls. *Photo by Bruce White.*

Above: Former ranger Rachel Storey and I pay a visit to Ranger Bruce White at Katahdin Stream Ranger Station. *Photo by Jennifer Smith Mayo.*

Below: Former ranger Rachel Storey, my Daicey Pond partner Charity Levasseur, and I have birthdays that fall very close together. Here we are turning a collective 120 years old. *Photo by Bruce White.*

Above: Search-and-rescue training often includes creating improvised carry systems, like this backpack I made out of 1.5-inch webbing. Ranger Bruce White and I once carried a hiker down the Hunt Trail with a similar setup. *Photo by Bruce White.*

Below: We work closely with the Maine Forest Service on rescue operations. Here we are during a training session, learning how best to communicate, signal, and support air crews from the ground. *Photo by Bruce White.*

Above: Maine's Air National Guard help the park with rescuing patients and moving supplies, like on this operation. *Photo by Spc. Adam Simmler, public domain on Wikimedia.*

Above: This old eastern white pine was struck by lightning last year and has subsequently dried out. We'll have to remove it soon. *Photo by the author.*

Above: One of the beauties of ranger work is the variety. On this day I was building picnic tables with a crew of rangers and volunteers. *Photo by Bruce White.*

Below: Late in the season, Charity (left) and I often find ourselves taking on major projects, such as roofing cabins with a crew of rangers. *Photo by Bruce White.*

Above: When the snows begin to arrive, we know it will soon be time to close. *Photo by the author.*

CHAPTER 10

My son Leo and I head up the hill to the campground, watching the top of Katahdin climb over the roof of the library. This is one of the few days I don't start at my desk, recording the weather, a sacrosanct task at Baxter Park. Almost nothing takes precedence over the "whether-you-like-it-or-not report," as Russell Pond ranger Brendan Curran used to call the day's forecast. Matagamon Gate broadcasts the outlook for the summit and the next few days at 7 A.M. whenever the park is open.

Because Baxter Park is one of the rare places left where the weather actually matters, it's important stuff. Campers rely on my scribbles to make their plans, and many head over as soon as I post the weather sheet on the kiosk beside the library, reading over my shoulder, still in their pajamas. Rain might mean a day with a book on the porch, a Scrabble session in the library, or a shortened hike rather than a daylong attempt at the big one. Weather is crucial.

At each duty station, rangers jot down the forecast as it comes over the scratchy radio. When the Matagamon gatekeeper finishes, reporting any additional notes or closures, stations "10-4" that they copied, one after another, all the way through the park. Matagamon signs off, and then I relay the whole thing to Kidney Pond and sometimes Katahdin Stream, because they both have a difficult time hearing the north end. The process can take fifteen minutes if the weather is variable, which it invariably is. This being northern Maine, we can have brilliant sun in the morning, showers in the afternoon, and heavy thunderstorms in the evening. Rain, snow, and hail all in the same day. Whatever the forecast, Katahdin has its own ideas about the weather it throws down its slopes.

This task is so vital at Baxter that I do nothing else until it's completed. If no one is at Kidney Pond, I drive over and post the weather there, too. Katahdin Stream does the same for Abol.

Not this morning, however. I unlock the station and go "10-8," letting the gate know I'm on duty, and then Leo and I close up and make for the waterfront just as Matagamon gatekeeper Marcia Anderson begins her meteorological spiel.

Today, we have other business.

We don life jackets and grab kayak paddles. Unlike his older brother, Gus, 10-year-old Leo isn't crazy about paddling, and he took some convincing, but he's game. I haul our two small rental kayaks over to the dock and help him into one. These are adult-size boats, and he barely fills the cockpit. When he shoves off, it looks more like wrestling than paddling at first. But he settles in and starts moving out into the pond.

"Which way, Dad?" he asks over his shoulder as I pull my boat out toward him. His life jacket gets stuck on the back of his seat, making a cowl around his head.

"We're going to do a circuit, counterclockwise, around the pond. Do you see anything?"

"Not yet."

We paddle quietly. Katahdin looms over the far shore, and as we get out onto the pond, Barren, Coe, OJI, and Doubletop mountains all loft up over the surrounding trees. It's a spectacular, sweeping view. Up close, swirling in the wake of my paddle, are the carcasses of green drakes, a mayfly that fish—and consequently anglers—love. They look a bit like the empty husks of earwigs floating on the surface. I often see gray tadpoles dart up to grab one and then instantly disappear into the dark, but not today.

Everything is peaceful.

"This is my job, bud," I say to Leo, who is drifting, taking it all in.

"I know," he says. At 10, he still thinks this ranger business is pretty cool.

It isn't long before we see what we're looking for. Even at 50 yards, its black body and profile are instantly recognizable as it quietly floats on the gentle waves.

Today, the third Saturday in July, is the Audubon Loon Count. From 7 to 7:30 A.M., birdwatchers across the state, and rangers across the park, take to their nearest body of water to survey the most beloved birds in the North Woods.

I've participated every year since I've been at Daicey and almost never get to log a count. A couple of years ago, I had two, but most years I paddle around the pond and disappointedly mark my map with a big zero. Some years, loons fly by on their way to other waters, calling their well-known yodel as they pass as if to taunt me.

Loons visit Daicey, but they don't breed on the pond. It's a bit too small and exposed for them. No islands or peninsulas provide cover, as they do over at Kidney. These famously vocal birds return to the same waters every year to breed, and they do so for a long time—some have been here below Katahdin longer than I have, living two decades or more. They deposit their camo-green eggs about the same time we rangers arrive in the spring, so there are enough weeks to try again if the first brood fails.

Kidney Pond is a much bigger basin, and almost every year there's at least one chick born on a nest on the island in the middle. These tiny fluff-balls ride on their parents' backs until they learn to dive and then, hopefully, soar. At the end of the season, we worry whether the little ones will be flying well enough to get off the pond before it's locked in with ice.

As Leo and I watch, the loon swims across the pond, then begins to flap and—it appears—run across the surface. It makes the longest diagonal it can on the compact basin and takes off, banking in a long arc around the cove at the shore most distant from the campground. The tiny shape loops around, with pines and spruce as a backdrop, then rises over the trees and shoots directly above us, focusing every bit of energy on lifting off. The dotted wings groan audibly as they flap over our heads.

"Isn't that wing whir cool?" I ask Leo.

"Yeah," he says quietly, staring up at the sky. He seems suitably impressed.

We continue around the pond but don't see any other loons. I'm grateful Leo and I got to see even one.

From the water, the campground appears more primitive than ever, and the perspective makes the cabins seem even smaller—like log cottages from another time preserved by some enchantment. Paddling toward them, it's easy to imagine that it's the seventeenth century and we're frontiersmen approaching a remote outpost. The noble twin pines that gave the old sporting camp here its name lord over everything else, graceful black-green branches reaching for the sun, arms out, always ready to dance.

We spot the soaring eastern white pine that got hit by lightning last year, near Cabin 9. It looks terrible, dried out and dying, bark falling off in great sheets, but that's what happens when you take a zillion volts.

"Did you know that lightning is hotter than the surface of the sun?" Leo asks when I point out the tree.

I allow as how I didn't know that, but it helps explain this tree. The sap inside fried and dried when it took the hit. The camper who was inside Cabin 9, not even 20 feet away, all but wet his pants. A science teacher, he walked me over to the tree when I came on duty a couple of days later and showed me how the current cut its way down the trunk, spiraling from one side to the other, searing off the bark and scarring the bole all along the 60-foot length of the tree.

Then he pointed out where it went through the roots on its way to the water, making furrows on the dark soil like a farmer with a hoe. He explained how the moss at the base of the tree exploded and pointed to big green chunks, like heads of lettuce, lying all over the place.

"I couldn't hear out of my left ear for a whole day afterward," he told me. "It gave me new respect for the power of lightning."

We could all do with a bit more respect for this truly awesome natural force. I used to be cavalier about lightning, not worrying too much when it was around. Then came the day during my fifth season when I found myself kneeling astride a 24-year-old kid from an island off Portland, trying to pump life back into him.

———————

I'd never been in a war zone, but I imagined that was what it felt like. The sky lit up by pummeling violence. Lightning bolts bursting through the dark like tracers. Artillery volleys of thunder pounding the valley, shaking the ground. This was like no storm I had ever seen before or have seen since. The lightning was so intense it was going around in circles, flashing every 30 seconds, followed instantly by deep, percussive wallops of thunder, the kind that vibrates walls and makes you instinctively duck your head down into your shoulders, as if that would help.

I'd spent the afternoon working on my new camp with roving ranger Rachel Storey. Rovers are rangers without assigned duty stations. They fill in at the park's ten campgrounds when rangers are on rare vacation days. When no one needs time off, they simply work on projects from a list they carry in the pocket of their BDUs. This might mean the less-than-exciting task of cleaning out roadside culverts. It might mean hiking into the backcountry to build canoe racks. Or it could involve a day of patrol on the mountain. Rovers travel all over the park and get to know every site.

I always thought it seemed like a cool gig until I learned that rover schedules fluctuate, and they never know where they might be heading until a day or two in advance. They also have to work at the gate, a sedentary position that I've always felt goes against the very idea of rangering. By definition, rangers are supposed to move about, not sit in a toll booth all day helping cranky incoming guests.

On that day, Rachel was giving me a hand cutting bunk beds in half for the log camp we had just finished building down in the field below Daicey Pond. The built-in bunks in the tiny volunteer camp where I had been staying wouldn't fit through the doorway of the new ranger housing, where they were going to be repurposed. I was quite keen on getting them inside for my 5-year-old son Gus to eventually sleep in. The park wanted them upstairs to provide quarters for rescuers and firefighters in case of extended searches or wildland blazes. Regardless, Rachel and I had the Sawzall out, making horizontal cuts on the 4-by-4 posts that married upper to lower bunk and transforming the beds into twin singles.

A boisterous 28-year-old, Rachel had been at the park for a couple of seasons, starting at the visitor center. She was always smiling and chattering and fun to be around, hair in Princess Leia buns, addressing everyone as "friend." She was game for most tasks within the park, intent on proving herself as a new ranger. With our ear protection on, we couldn't hear each other, but that didn't give her pause, and I could see her talking away as I pulled the trigger on the reciprocating saw. After working for a while in the stifling confines of Cozy Cabin (the park's name for the single-room building), we took a break, stepping outside in search of cool air.

It was very late on a muggy August afternoon, temperature and humidity both in the 80s, the kind of day where your T-shirt serves only to mop sweat. At least mine.

Sitting on the stoop, we watched the sky over the AT morph into dense, menacing black clouds that blotted out the day's last remnants of sun. A movie couldn't depict a gathering of evil any better. Soon, thunder rumbled across the Nesowadnehunk Valley, and lightning rent the skies over Katahdin.

Then it was upon us. Raindrops the size of .22-caliber bullets began to pelt the metal roof of the building. Lightning strikes streaked down like howitzer shells, accompanied by thunder rumbling the ground. I could feel the concussions in my feet and chest. The sky lit up like noontime then went dark, like a kid was flicking a celestial light switch over and over. I couldn't remember a storm so powerful.

I turned to talk to Rachel just as a flash-boom detonated over the horizon. It was such a rush of violent energy it all but knocked us over, and we both jumped.

"Man!" Rachel said. "That wasn't far away."

We huddled just inside the door of Cozy Cabin, watching trees bend in the wind and listening to rain thrash the roof.

Then the handheld on the windowsill screamed to life. "Man down, Katahdin Stream! I've got a man down!" It was Bruce White, typically unflappable, and it sounded bad.

Rachel and I raced for the truck. She hopped in the driver's seat, I grabbed the radio. "77, 79 en route to Katahdin Stream." Rachel gunned it out of the parking lot, tires spinning, wipers blazing.

———

The 2-mile drive was a blur of blackness and rain. The radio crackled away below the dash—several other units responded that they, too, were on the way. The ranking ranger for the evening, Mike Martin, was new to his role of evening duty officer, only recently returned from the Maine Criminal Justice Academy. I heard him ask the gate for information, what happened and where. A lot of people on the radio seemed to assume that the strike happened up on the shoulders of Katahdin, somewhere at elevation—a logical thought. I triggered the mic. Sometimes I take an extra breath so I won't seem nervous on the radio in an emergency, but I felt a strange calm settle over me, as if watching myself from the outside.

"Go ahead, Andy."

"Mike, it's at Katahdin Stream. Bruce has a man down in the campground."

"10-4. Thanks."

Rachel made the hard left into Katahdin Stream Campground, and we scanned for activity at the lean-tos by the stream whenever bolts lit up the sky. Nothing seemed unusual. The sites were quiet as people took shelter inside. Then we heard someone else on the radio—Charity?—say the patient was at the walk-in sites just across the bridge.

The storm seemed to be circling back around, its progress blocked by the high wall of Katahdin, as we parked the truck at the edge of the road. Rain was still pouring down ferociously. Charity was at the side of the road with the hood of her raincoat up over her face. She pointed down the wide path toward the walk-in sites.

"Lean-to 3," she said. We ran for it, my headlamp turning the old woods road into a soggy, black tunnel as thunder boomed.

These walk-in sites are where ambitious campers, those who don't mind carrying their gear a ways, find some of the most peaceful camping spots in the south end of the park. A handful of tent campsites and open-faced lean-tos hunker by the fast-moving stream, separated by dense thickets of mixed woods, providing the kind of privacy that is hard to find in most other campgrounds in the park.

When we arrived at Lean-to 3, Bruce and Ranger Dean Levasseur were administering CPR on the worn boards of the lean-to, the AED (automatic external defibrillator) imploring them to pump. Several campers stood at the edge of the dirt campsite. Acute stress reaction—what I used to call "shock" before learning that shock is actually a blood-flow problem—was written all over their faces.

A robotic voice commanded, *"Press, press, press, press."*

The patient was a big kid in his early 20s, with curly hair, his barrel chest bared to accommodate the AED leads. Vomit was all over his torso and the sleeping platform. Yes, even the pulseless can puke. The invasive nature of CPR—air forced into the lungs and sometimes the stomach—often causes patients to regurgitate the contents of their belly.

A woman stood nearby, saying, "Come on, baby. Come on."

"Press, press, press, press . . ."

Rachel and I saw another patient, sitting at the picnic table with his chin on his knees and arms around his legs, rocking back and forth. His shins look like peeled birch trees. We stepped over to him.

"Hey," I said, kneeling down.

"I'm Ranger Andrew, this is Ranger Rachel, and we're here to help."

He raised his head and stared blankly at the two of us. He appeared to be in his late teens.

"Help my brother," he said.

"We have plenty of rangers helping him," Rachel replied. "Let's have a look at you."

"HELP MY BROTHER!" he screamed in our faces, putting his head back down. We stepped away to do what he said.

"Press, press, press, press . . ."

The rain let up a little, and the thunder sounded like it was moving off. We heard reports coming in across the radio: a car was in a ditch up near Nesowadnehunk; fallen trees barricaded the park road; a trio of late hikers was still up on the mountain inside those anvil clouds. "It's like the devil himself walked into Baxter Park," one ranger commented.

Confusion continued as to what was going on at Katahdin Stream, so I gathered as many details as I could and radioed the gate to get an ambulance inbound.

"77 to Togue."

Gail picked up right away. She knew there was an emergency.

"Go ahead, 77."

"We have a lightning strike, 24-year-old male, unresponsive, CPR underway . . ."

I often say that Baxter State Park feels like an island. The southernmost edge is an hour removed from the closest grocery store and the nearest service station and 60 miles from a regional trauma center. If I forget something on my way to the cabin for my weekly shift, I go without. When Percival Baxter donated his "magnificent obsession," these woods and lakes around Maine's highest peak, he mandated that the park bearing his name should remain "forever wild," and it never seems more remote than when you're waiting for an ambulance.

As I talked into my handheld, observing the scene, I noticed the same sensation I had felt in the truck. It was as if I were watching myself scurrying about—radioing, running to get an oxygen tank, finding the right fitting in our O_2 bag—from somewhere above my head. Like my soul had drifted up and was looking back down.

"Press, press, press, press . . ."

"Andy," Rob Tice called from the lean-to platform, motioning for me to approach. One of the ranking rangers, he'd been administering oxygen and checking for a pulse. "You ready to take over compressions? Dean could use a rest."

I climbed onto the platform on my hands and knees, and the crew shifted to make room. Lean-to 3 accommodates four campers, and it felt cramped with Bruce, Rob, Dean, the patient, and me. I straddled the strike victim, knotted my hands, and began rocking down on his chest, finding the rhythm of the AED.

"Press, press, press, press . . ."

The kid beneath me seemed huge—and lifeless. His skin was getting pale, and bubbles formed at his lips as I heaved on his sternum. Hunched over, knees on either side of him like a playground bully, I pumped and pumped and pumped and pumped.

"Press, press, press, press . . ."

Chest compressions are exhausting work, but I knew I couldn't stop.

"Stand back," the AED finally told us. *"Do not touch the patient. Analyzing rhythm."*

I slumped, crawling back a few feet deeper into the lean-to, breathing heavily, my head bumping the sharply sloped roof. The little machine paused as it assessed the kid's internal electricity, and we waited, hoping this time it would deliver the shock that brought him back.

Come on, I thought. *Come on.*

————

Every year in our wilderness medical training we sit through lectures on both lightning safety and the relative ineffectiveness of CPR. Despite that overall ineffectiveness, instructors always mention that the situations where cardiopulmonary resuscitation proves most worthwhile are lightning strikes and drowning. In these heart-stopping instances, the body has its best chance of coming back.

The odds are good, too. By some estimates, more than 90 percent of people struck by lightning survive. In the United States, fishing leads to the most lightning accidents for obvious reasons. Anglers are often in boats, far from shore, and they're usually the tallest things around. Between 30 and 50 people get struck across the country in a typical year.

Lightning can cause untold damage to a person's insides, burning organs, frying nerves, tearing blood vessels, exploding bones. An instant billion volts, reaching temperatures five times hotter than the surface of the sun, can ignite your clothes, boil your sweat, and blow off your shoes. Survivors often suffer permanent injuries to their nervous system—our electrical wiring doesn't include a circuit breaker. The most common way lightning kills, however, is simply by halting the heart.

(Incidentally, the Guinness World Record holder for being struck by lightning is a park ranger, Roy Sullivan, from Shenandoah National Park, who was hit seven times across the length of his career. At Baxter Park, Ranger Mark Varney's station in Nesowadnehunk Field was hit twice. Thankfully, he was never struck himself.)

"*Continue CPR*," the AED said, bringing me back to the moment. In other words, the machine had found no shockable rhythm. Our heads dropped. I climbed back up onto the patient and renewed compressions.

"*Press, press, press, press . . .*"

The woman hovering over the patient chanted, "Come on, honey. Please."

I started to flag, and Rob tapped me on the shoulder. I crawled to the dark corner of the lean-to, making room. Another ranger began the same aggressive, elbows-locked, fist-on-sternum thrusting.

"*Press, press, press, press . . .*"

I climbed out of the lean-to and stepped to the side to catch my breath and wait.

Rescues often involve a lot of waiting. You wait for vitals checks. You wait while the lead reassures and comforts the patient. You wait for supplies to come up the trail. You wait for enough resources to arrive to begin an extraction. You wait to hear if a helicopter is available and then wait to hear its telltale heartbeat over the treetops.

In this case, as the skies opened and the patient lay on his back on the hard boards of the lean-to, eyes staring into the rafters, we waited for the AED to shock his heart into rhythm. Every minute that it didn't was hard to bear.

"*Stand back*," the AED said again. "*Do not touch the patient. Analyzing rhythm.*"

We stayed clear, hoping.

Then the compressions began again.

"*Press, press, press, press . . .*"

"That's the mother," someone whispered in my ear, eyes on the woman imploring her baby to come back.

Mike Martin, the man in charge of the park for the evening, arrived, and I filled him in. Like any good duty officer, he allowed the team to continue without interruption. Technically, he outranked all of us and could start throwing his weight around, especially in a life-or-death situation. To his credit, he didn't. In wilderness rescue, the first person on the scene is in charge until that person relinquishes responsibility to someone with superior medical training. In this case, we were all roughly on par. Both Bruce and Rob had been EMTs; most of us had years of Wilderness Medical Associates training. We'd all taken countless CPR courses.

"*Press, press, press, press . . .*"

This wasn't even Bruce's first lightning strike. He had been there 17 years ago—on almost the same day of the year—when a bolt hit a Boy Scout on the Knife Edge. The 13-year-old hiker was part of a troop of ten scouts and two leaders traversing Katahdin's famously exposed arête. Between 4 and 8 feet wide, with 1,000-foot drops on either side, the trail left them no place to go, and they were pinned by lightning when a sudden, unpredicted storm materialized. All members of the group felt the jolt. Ranger Esther Hendrickson climbed to the scene during the squall and provided care. One scout was killed instantly; another had severe burns and was airlifted by the Maine Air National Guard to Millinocket Regional Hospital the next morning.

In 1968, the park had a lightning fatality when a strike hit a group of 22 campers at Chimney Pond, stopping one man's heart. Another man had the pattern of the metal zipper of his sleeping bag immediately cauterized into his leg.

When I was stationed at Katahdin Stream, I had a few lightning-related incidents, but none with deadly consequences. On two different occasions, hikers told me they'd seen blue electricity arcing between their fingers while climbing the mountain in a thunderstorm. Another time, a goofy AT thru-hiker told me he'd been on the long plateau of the Tableland when a strike hit so close to him it made his mop of hair stand up and blew the Snickers bar right out of his hand. He thought it was kinda neat.

None of us felt that this evening was neat in any way.

Mike observed and did his best to coordinate the response, letting the CPR crew perform chest compressions and rescue breathing, keeping Charity on the road so the ambulance crew from Millinocket would know where to turn, and checking with the gate to see if the bus we had all been willing to arrive had entered the park.

"Not yet," said Gail, concern in her voice.

"*Press, press, press, press . . .*"

Suddenly a ranger yelled, "I have a pulse!"

CHAPTER 11

"54 TO DAICEY POND."

I'm doing my chores on an early August morning—already a warm 70 degrees by 9 A.M. with a full-bore sun in the blue overhead—when my radio squawks in my pocket. I used to carry my little Motorola handheld in the back pocket of my BDUs, and I liked to joke that I was talking out my ass. It's much more comfortable in the side of our new tactical pants, and I'm less likely to bump it against things. (One of my ongoing fears is that it gets triggered and everyone in the park can hear me talking to myself.) A dark army-green, these park-issued pants have a compartment seemingly every inch. Pockets literally within pockets, designed for extra clips and knives, phones and handcuffs. Mine carry a multitool, a flashlight, keys to the truck, the radio, often screws and nails from the current project I'm working on, and usually whatever litter I find on the ground.

"10-3," I say.

"Andy, can you go down to your parking lot and look for a vehicle registered to Burns?" Bruce asks. "I caught a couple of guys with backpacks who wanted to climb this morning at Katahdin Stream. I told them the mountain was closed. They said they were going to hike back to their car. Said it's parked in your lot. I'm on my way in."

Happy for a distraction from cleaning toilets, I jog down to the day-use lot to check the handful of cars and trucks parked there, stretching myself across hoods to read the gate pass on the dash of each one.

At Baxter Park, we regulate the number of hikers on the mountain by the number of vehicles we let in each morning. On a clear August Saturday like this one, cars sit in a long line at Togue Pond Gate, most headed to a Katahdin trailhead.

It's such a popular destination that when I arrive for my shift late on Friday evening, I'll often see people parked in front of the big barrier at the south end. The occupants sleep in their vehicles, technically illegally camping, and wait for the gate staff to pull the pin and swing the wide beams open at 6 A.M. The queue in the morning can stretch a half-mile or more, and the parking lots at the Katahdin trailheads—Abol, Katahdin Stream, and Roaring Brook—fill by 7:15. Once that happens, we close the mountain to hiking, turning away any latecomers. This is the only way to preserve the wilderness experience. Even so, on high-summer days like today, the summit of Katahdin can feel like a convention or a busy train station with people arriving from every direction and standing around en masse.

To keep numbers manageable, to preserve and protect the peak from the effect of all those humans—preservation, remember, is first on our mission statement, recreation a distant second—and to give ourselves a chance at rescuing those who need help, we simply have to limit climbing.

Every Saturday the gatekeepers and frontcountry rangers are verbally abused by people who think it's their inalienable right to climb Maine's highest peak whenever they feel like it. Many drive hours or days to get here without doing any research first, so they are dumbfounded and pissed when they hit the gate and are told the mountain is closed for the day. We began selling day-use parking reservations several years ago to help alleviate the situation, but we still take a rash from a lot of angry customers. No one gets it worse than Saturday morning gatekeepers.

Even after being told the mountain is closed, many hikers decide they're going to climb anyway, like this Burns party. They find a place to park their vehicles—on the side of the road, in front of an outhouse, in a camper's spot, at the long-distance shelter, at a lot for another trail—and set off. This year, I've seen an increase of vehicles parking at Daicey Pond and hiking the AT 2.5 miles over to Katahdin Stream to ascend the Hunt Trail, adding 5 miles to their already long day.

I don't see the Burns vehicle in the lot, and I turn to the hiking roster to check there. Nothing. I'm scanning the list of names scrawled on the sheet when Bruce barrels in, big clouds of dust enveloping his pickup. He looks perturbed, freckles redder than usual.

"Anything?" he asks, climbing out of his truck.

"Negative."

"Well, these guys said they parked here. They also said they camped beside the stream at Daicey Pond last night."

I was not on duty last night so I couldn't be sure they didn't park on the front lawn of the library.

Bruce double-checks the gate passes. Nothing. We decide they probably came up the AT from where it enters the park at Abol Bridge. "I'm gonna head there and see what I can find," he tells me, climbing back behind the wheel.

"Doesn't look like we're going to get to the water line at Kidney this morning?" I ask. Kidney Pond Campground's water source, Jackson Brook, evaporated in the August heat, leaving the two rangers stationed there dry. Bruce and I were going to try to get a new line from Rocky Pond to work.

"Doesn't look like it," he says.

While we're talking, Dawson, our Appalachian Trail steward, radios in. The park funds this "ridge running" position to ameliorate some of the problems that walk into Baxter dressed as thru-hikers. A recent high school grad from the nearby woods hamlet of Mount Chase, our current steward is in the area cutting blowdowns. He's a sharp kid who worked stints on trail crews during summers, and like me, always wanted to work in the park. Bruce tells him to start hiking toward Katahdin Stream Campground and keep an eye out for two young guys with big packs. At first, he's confused. Still a probie, Dawson hasn't yet chased AT hikers all over like Bruce and I.

"Just to confirm," he says, "you want me to hike *back* toward Katahdin Stream?" He sounds like he's just over the hill from Daicey.

"Correct. See if you can locate these two guys we're looking for."

"10-4."

Within twenty minutes, our intrepid steward has caught up to the party in question.

"6-22 to 54," he whispers into his radio, excited. Bruce and I chuckle, but he's doing exactly the right thing. "I have eyes on. They are turning around toward Daicey Pond."

"Keep following them," Bruce tells him.

A few minutes later, Dawson is back with another update, again in hushed tones. "We're at the juncture of the Grassy Pond and Daicey Nature trails." He sounds like a tween up past his bedtime talking on his phone even though he's not supposed to. We have to turn up our radios to hear him.

Bruce and I look at each other and chuckle some more.

The location instantly clarifies things: the two hikers are trying to avoid detection by skirting staffed campgrounds, and they are undoubtedly making for Abol Bridge, just as we guessed. By now district ranger Rob Tice has joined us. He's a little bit younger than me and returned to the park from the police academy at roughly the same time I started my Baxter career. We figure it's time to let Dawson collar the pair. Otherwise they could simply take a left onto Lost Pond Trail and escape.

"Go ahead and tell them someone wants to talk to them at the Daicey Pond parking lot," Rob explains over the radio.

Twenty minutes later the three of them appear. The two guys are hipsters in their early 20s with requisite beards and trucker caps. They sport two days of grime on their fronts and full packs on their backs. Rob steps over and quietly begins to question them. With three park trucks in the lot and four rangers, the situation is beginning to seem like an event, and many hikers have one ear to the scene.

Ranger Tice asks the duo if they bothered to register when they came into the park. Baxter allows backpackers to enter outside the traditional gate system, where most campers get their passes and permits, so long as they register at the nearest opportunity. The shorter, longer-haired fellow tells us they did. Then he looks down at his boots and says, "Under a pseudonym." Rob, wearing his duty vest and sidearm, presses him.

"It was Mike something," the kid says.

The pair are beginning to squirm, obviously ruing their decisions. Illegal hiking and stealth camping seem like great fun—until you get caught. Rob has them sit on a rock while he writes up their citations, one each for illegal camping and failure to register. They're looking at as much as $1,000 for their efforts.

Dawson, Bruce, and I chat off to the side. Our young AT steward doesn't usually say much, but this adventure has him carrying on like a kid who's had too much candy. He tells us he overheard one of the guys say, "Those questions from the other ranger really got my adrenalin going."

Bruce grins. Nobody will give you more help if you need it in Baxter Park than Bruce White. I've seen him wait for hours with disabled vehicles, stop in town to pick up supplies for campers he's never met before, spend half a day trying to fix something for someone. But nobody wants to nail the baddies that despoil the park more, either. We joke with Dawson that he better get used to chasing down bad guys. We regale him with tales of stakeouts, pinches, and late-night treks to extinguish campfires started by outlaws, many of them thru-hikers.

———————

The Appalachian Trail has had an uneasy relationship with Baxter State Park ever since it was created in 1937, six years after the founding of the park. The nascent AT actually predated the establishment of Baxter Park, however, because the first designated section, incorporating the Katahdin area, was cut in 1886 and ran from the summit to Kidney Pond. A project of the Appalachian Mountain Club, the trail was a known entity when Governor Baxter purchased and set aside the mountain for the people of Maine in 1931, and he welcomed AT involvement in his new park. He wrote to the initial trailblazers: "I am pleased to learn that the Appalachian

Trail has been marked right through to Katahdin, and of course I have no objection to having your trail signs placed on the land that I have conveyed to the State. In fact, I am pleased that this has been done."

But tensions eventually rose in the relationship. Ironically, it was Appalachian Trail Conservancy (ATC) leader and trail visionary Myron Avery who was bothered by the AT in and around the park. The ATC itself complained about hiker behavior, damage to the landscape, and the volume of foot traffic to the area, according to one history. Things really came to a head, though, when Avery backed an initiative to subsume Baxter's park into a national park centered on Katahdin. The governor welcomed federal involvement in the form of crews from the Civilian Conservation Corps building lean-tos and trails, but he opposed a National Park Service takeover on every level, fearing paved roads, big lodges, and huge crowds.

Despite their differences, Baxter and Avery wanted basically the same thing—to preserve Katahdin and its magnificent surroundings. By the time I put on the uniform, it was the thru-hikers themselves, or at least a misbehaving subset, who were creating the biggest disturbance. They camped wherever they felt like, they gathered in groups of 40 or more (against regulations), they partied, they littered. They even had a fraternity called Riff Raff that existed so members could throw massive bashes, like their college counterparts.

In 2014, then–park director Jensen Bissell wrote an open letter to the ATC expressing his frustration with the situation. That year 2,017 thru-hikers registered at the park. Many more likely visited but didn't bother to check in. Bissell mentioned the difficulties this group caused, such as bringing in dogs, using controlled substances on the summit, and simply overcrowding Baxter's campgrounds. He intimated that the AT didn't have to end on Katahdin and that if changes weren't made, then "relocating key trail portions or the trail terminus would be another option."

The letter caused quite a stir, igniting a firestorm of debate on the internet. The next summer I met a few people from the ATC who were sent north in an attempt to smooth things over. The ATC decided to open an information center in Monson, the last town thru-hikers visit before entering the Hundred Mile Wilderness that deposits them at the southwest corner of Baxter Park, to help educate hikers before they reach the park.

At Katahdin Stream, which many call the "Grand Central Station" of Baxter, day-hikers fill the parking lot by 7:15 A.M. almost any morning the sun shines, and they're joined by a steady stream of AT hikers, finishing their epic odyssey from Springer Mountain, Georgia. One of the many duties of the Katahdin Stream rangers is to register all these long-distance hikers and to oversee their camping area, the Birches. It's not uncommon to drive up to the ranger station and to see a snaking line of grubby backpackers, their hair unruly and their gear in tatters. By the time they reach Baxter Park, many look like the hobos or tramps of yore.

Extraordinary people are among this crowd. Some of the finest campers I've ever met were AT thru-hikers.

I remember a Swedish family who traveled the trail as a foursome: mom, dad, and two kids not yet in grade school. These folks were on their way down the mountain after the exhausting and emotional completion of their thru-hike when they came across an injured hiker. The father sprinted down to alert the ranger on duty and then ran back up with supplies.

A woman with the trail name Moon Pie invited me to come eat Moon Pies when the company that makes these chocolate-covered delicacies surprised her with a case to celebrate the end of her journey. A group of ex-military guys came upon a climber who had dislocated her shoulder and performed an impromptu rescue, helping her all the way down. I could go on and on with examples of AT thru-hiker kindness.

I'm particularly impressed with the combat vets who use the trail as a way to decompress after their wartime experience. The tradition dates back to the first confirmed thru-hiker, Earl Shaffer, who was a radio man in the Pacific during World War II and "walked off the war" by trekking from Georgia to Maine.

The vet community has grown dramatically since I started, with continued U.S. involvement in Iraq and Afghanistan, and I had the good fortune to accompany a group sponsored by Warrior Hike a few years back as they finished their journey. Founded by a marine who hiked the trail after his deployment and found the quiet and solitude very therapeutic, the organization provides gear and logistical support to allow soldiers to do the trail with few cares. It wasn't *therapeutic* for me, huffing along trying to keep up with some of the most fit humans on the planet, but it was a fun and memorable day.

For all these good AT hikers, we see our share of wannabe outlaws. We get BOLOs—be on the lookout for—about AT hikers every year from other agencies along the trail. This one has been intimidating women. That one has a warrant out back home. This one has a firearm. That one has been stealing. Many people forget that the Appalachian Trail serves as the dark woods at the end of the street in a lot of the Eastern Megalopolis, and, unfortunately, crime finds its way onto the trail.

I've combed through the woods looking for plenty of thru-hikers. I've caught AT hikers bivouacking in the parking lot at Katahdin Stream and camping in the field by my camp at Daicey Pond. I've kicked squatters out of the Daicey Library, and Charity busted a pair who attempted to pitch a tent in our picnic area within full view of the ranger station. I evicted a vagrant who took a taxi into the park with a box overflowing with hard liquor, to party with the hikers. And I've collared all kinds of thru-hikers for ditching their trash at their sites. In my second season, my supervisor even had me change into civilian clothes to stake out a group to see if I could find out any intel on one in particular we were on the lookout for. No dice.

When I started, I was surprised by all this. I naively assumed that the most hardcore backpackers would be true environmentalists, having come to appreciate the nation's wildlands as they walked through them. But this is not the case. Sure, some think this way, but many others are using the trail as something to do while they figure out what they're supposed to do with their lives; they couldn't give a shit about conservation.

A few years back, Baxter Park was involved in the famous case of long-distance trail runner Scott Jurek, who made national headlines for willfully ignoring a bunch of park rules and regulations that he thought did not apply to him, despite telling rangers he would comply. The park fined him for public drinking, littering, and gathering in an oversized group. Most park visitors who climbed that day did so for the natural beauty and wilderness experience, and instead they found a circus of advertisements and partying at the summit. When asked to tone it down, the thru-hikers refused. This sense of entitlement seems common, especially among younger people, and it seems to grow as northbound hikers approach the end of their journey. It is indisputably an impressive accomplishment: hiking most of the East Coast, seeing the country on foot, spending five or six months living out of a backpack.

I used to think I'd like to thru-hike the AT. I really love the liberating feeling of having everything I need to survive on my back, like I can go anywhere and do anything. At least, I thought that until I began working as a park ranger on the trail.

First, there are simply too many people these days. We see thousands each season. Many that we meet seem to think finishing the trail makes them uniquely special, as if we haven't seen literally tens of thousands like them before.

A lot of thru-hikers are offended that we charge $10 a night to stay at the park and think they should be allowed to camp for free, as they can for much of the rest of the way. We get a lot of attitude. Websites are filled with directions on how and where to camp illegally in Baxter State Park. Some hikers claim to not have any money when they check in at Katahdin Stream, and all of us who work along the trail in the park have driven a thru-hiker to the park boundary. Upon the threat of eviction, most of these individuals discover that they had some cash in their socks after all.

———

Our trail steward Dawson's morning adventure took place along a stretch of the AT that's no stranger to bad behavior. Bruce and I have pinched several parties along its length over the years, including our famous "Navy SEAL" raid, which took place years ago on a warm June night. Bruce happened to be sitting in one of the guest chairs in my office, hanging out as we often did when we were both seasonals, when a fisherman stepped in. He'd closed the pond, so to speak, working a line in the water until he could hardly see. Daicey is known as an evening fishery, its brook trout hungriest after sundown, and many anglers walk off without a bite because they don't wait long enough.

This fellow was a local well versed in trout behavior. A radiologist at Millinocket Hospital who explored the depths whenever he wasn't exploring someone's innards, he was a friend of one of my former Daicey partners and a regular on the pond. He never let a little darkness get between him and a fish.

"Are there supposed to be lights on the far side of the pond?" he asked.

"Nope," I said. "See some?"

"Yeah, there are lights strung up in the trees over near where the Grassy Pond Trail comes in."

"Interesting . . . thanks for the tip."

Bruce looked at me.

"Feel like going for a paddle?"

He knew he didn't even need to ask.

We made for the door. Outside, the moon had risen over the right shoulder of Katahdin and was raining a silvery glow across the still pond. Bruce tried to reach the evening's duty officer, but he was dealing with some issue on the other side of the mountain and couldn't hear us. The few clouds above were backlit against the gray sky as we very quietly put a canoe in, me in the bow, Bruce in the stern. We J-stroked our way out into the middle of Daicey, our paddles never leaving the water in order to make as little noise as possible.

"Rachel's gonna be jealous I went on a moonlight paddle with you and not her," Bruce whispered.

"Don't get any ideas."

Halfway across the pond we could see what looked like a string of white Christmas lights suspended in the trees just off Grassy Pond Trail. We quickly crossed the rest of the way across the spring-fed basin, and

Bruce steered us into the far cove on the pond's east side. I silently put down my paddle and slid over the gunwale into the waist-deep water.

"What the hell are you doing?" Bruce whispered. His eyes were wide in the moonlight, and he was trying not to crack up. "I could have paddled you over to the pullout."

"Navy SEAL," I said, and he had a hard time not laughing out loud. "I'm gonna rub some mud on my cheeks and put some twigs in my hat."

I began to thread through the huckleberry bushes as quietly as one could thread through dead bushes.

"Yeah, you're a real commando," Bruce said. He put his head down, chuckling into his lap, trying to stifle the noise. "Navy SEAL? More like a wounded moose."

I checked to make sure I had a flashlight and shuffled my way across the bottom, stumbling over submerged rocks. I almost fell a couple of times, getting my shirt wet in the process. Splashes echoed across the small pond, and I was certain the campers must have heard me, but I staggered onto Daicey Pond Nature Trail and composed myself. This narrow path wound all the way around the pond, and it would take me just where I needed to go. A century of boots and erosion had ground the dirt away to expose rocks in the trail, and I aimed for those as best I could to avoid snapping twigs. I figured if the campers had heard me, haste was critical at that point.

The moonlight gave me just enough illumination to make out the path. I trotted along the narrow walkway, and my heart was pumping by the time I turned left onto Grassy Pond Trail. I squatted down and looked ahead. I could see the lights wound through the branches just off the trail. These stealth campers were not the first to bivouac on this little mossy shelf above the pond, but with all these lights, I thought they might be the dimmest.

I could make out two male voices. Probably southbound thru-hikers too tired to make it the 6 miles out of the park after climbing the mountain. This happened all the time. I jogged up the trail toward them as quietly as possible. As I got closer, I could see the pair in the restaurant-like glow of the lights. Two fit, middle-aged men were chatting happily away, oblivious to my presence, pulling gear out of stuff sacks and getting ready to turn in for the night. They already had their two-person tent set up in a little clearing. One of them paused, his head tilted up, like a whitetail alert for danger. I stopped. I didn't want them to have a chance to run.

When they went back to work, I stepped into the clearing and turned my big Maglite on them. Their initial reaction was gratifying—both jumped and startled like a couple of cartoon characters. Then they turned angrily toward me, and I braced myself. But when they saw the badge, their shoulders slumped and their expressions told me they knew what they were doing was wrong.

"Hey guys, ranger here to get you checked in."

They stared blankly.

"You know you're supposed to camp in designated sites in Baxter Park, correct?" I asked.

"Yes, sir."

"Do you see any site designation here? A sign, firepit, picnic table?"

"No, sir."

"That's because this is not a camping spot. This is an *illegal* camping spot. You're going to have to come with me."

By that time, Bruce had huffed into camp.

"Take your tent down and pack up your stuff," I told them.

Bruce and I stepped to the side to confer. We decided to move them to the Birches. Typically, only northbound thru-hikers were allowed to use the site's two lean-tos and tent platform, on the theory that they would have had a difficult time making a reservation trekking north in the woods. But if we attempted to throw these guys out, forcing them to hike down and across the boundary line, like we have done with so many others over the years, they'd likely just stealth camp somewhere along the Penobscot in the southernmost quadrant of the park because it was so late. Besides, we had an idea for these two.

"Hike them around the pond," Bruce said to me. "I'll paddle the canoe back, we'll throw their stuff into the back of my truck, and I'll drive them to the Birches."

The two gentlemen got their packs ready, and we hiked back the way I had just come. They explained to me, as I hiked behind them, my boots squishing with every step, that my hunch was correct, and they were exhausted SOBOs (southbound thru-hikers), a couple of Midwesterners recently retired from the air force, who didn't have enough remaining energy to hike out.

"Why didn't you just get a site at Katahdin Stream and kick up your feet?" I asked.

"Probably should have."

"Well, that would have cost you twenty bucks rather than the hundreds in fines you're facing now."

They went quiet.

We followed the AT around the pond. Water squirted up between my toes with every step. I wondered whether the boots of Navy SEALs squished when they made landfall. They must.

The bright moon made our headlamps almost unnecessary, giving the trees a silver haze and throwing shadows behind every trunk. It was like walking into a photo negative or hiking in an Ansel Adams landscape. We finally went down the steep hill into the Daicey Pond day-use parking lot and met Bruce. We heaved the guys' big packs into the truck bed, and they followed, settling beside the wheel wells. Bruce hauled them to the Birches, and in the morning, they got a juicy fine for illegal camping.

We could have just thrown them out, rather than providing accommodation for the evening. This way, however, they hiked down the trail, telling their story to all the NOBOs they met, warning them about what happens when you stealth camp in Baxter Park.

CHAPTER 12

"So, let me get this straight—you are the guy who climbs mountains in the dark? When it's raining? When it's frozen? Carrying litters down rocky slopes lit only by a headlamp? Bushwhacking off-trail at midnight? And you sprained your knee coming down the steps of a fancy restaurant in Rochester, New York?"

"10-4."

"That's hilarious," Bruce says, chuckling. "Hilarious."

Then all serious: "I'm going to need to see a note from your doctor."

I'd just returned from delivering my older son, Gus, to the University of Rochester for his freshman semester. This was difficult for all of us, none more so than my other boy, Leo, who fretted for months about seeing his big brother go. "This is the last [insert event] we'll do with Gus," he'd say again and again. We were all sad to think that he'd no longer be living with us.

Gus grew up spending shifts with me at Baxter Park during summers, from infancy to adulthood, and now Bruce, who had built him a sandbox at Katahdin Stream when he was still toddling, reminded me of all the times he would pass my wife, Lisa, on the way out of the park, with a sobbing little blond guy in the backseat who didn't want to leave. "Now it's Dad who's going to be doing the crying on the way home," he laughed.

After moving Gus into his room, we took him out for a celebratory dinner at an upscale eatery we'd found when looking at the school. We had a nice meal on a rooftop, surrounded by Rochester's hipoisie. I excused myself to visit the restroom and stepped from the glaring sunshine into the dark interior. My eyes didn't adjust in time for me to see there were four steps on the stairs, not the two I'd anticipated. My right leg came down hard and twisted at the knee. No pops or cracks, just a lot of pain.

My doc, a guy not much older than me, who'd relocated from Texas to Belfast, Maine, called it a "lateral collateral knee sprain." I explained that the knee had been aching for much of the summer, especially when climbing.

"If it keeps bothering you, the next step is to do an MRI," he said, noting he didn't want me walking on "uneven ground."

"That's basically all ground where I work."

"Yeah," he said. "I'm writing you a note." He scrawled on a pad, specifying three days off for recuperating.

Injuries are nothing new to park rangers. This season alone, my feet went out from under me on the great slab at Katahdin Stream Falls, slamming me onto my back and elbow. I fell twice crossing Katahdin Stream, tearing open my left shin one time. I've been stabbed by nails and scraped by trees, and I've twisted most of my lower body parts. Tennis elbow from chain sawing; back strain and retinal tear from heavy lifting; bruised toes from dropped firewood. Luckily, I've never been seriously hurt.

Some of my colleagues, on the other hand . . .

I once raced over to Kidney Pond when Ranger Dean Levasseur called and asked for my help "right away." I'd worked with him long enough to know it was serious. I was also aware he had just been to headquarters to pick up a table saw. My mind was picturing ugly, arterial-squirting scenarios. I covered the ground faster than was advisable only to find him with his feet up in the ranger station, gauze held to his nose. He appeared to have all his appendages and their requisite digits.

"I was pulling a nail out of Cabin 7 at eye level," he told me, "and whacked myself good. I thought I broke my nose and was going to need a ride to the hospital." He pulled his hand away to show me, and sure enough he had a little clawhammer *V* right between the eyes. His wife, Charity, appeared a few minutes later, breathless, having picked up the radio call while she was hiking. He would wear a bruise for a few days but was fine.

Dean was prone to these sorts of odd occurrences. When he transferred from Abol to Kidney, where we worked closely together on the same shift, I was wary because of his reputation for being unlucky. This was the guy who, in his first week working for the park at the gate, had a couple of hikers walk up and present him with a jawbone.

"We found this," they said.

"Looks like it's from a bear," he said.

"It's not from a bear."

"How do you know?"

"Because that bear would have to have a very good dentist." They pointed out a filling.

Turned out the mandible came from a gentleman who had moved into a tent just outside the park in the off-season and had likely done himself in. Coyotes found the corpse and dragged the bones around, leaving this one near a popular bivouac for late-arriving campers.

Dean was also on duty when another suicidal individual decided to remove half of his cranium with a shotgun on Elbow Pond Trail for all to see. Two little boys found the body and reported it to the rangers at Kidney. I had just gone off duty and was on my way out of the park, oblivious, as a handful of frontcountry staff hiked in to the gruesome scene.

And then there was the time when Dean was stationed on the east side and frantic parents called him over to their Roaring Brook site: "Something's wrong with our baby!" The couple was helplessly watching as their toddler turned blue, in serious distress. The mother was distraught, crying. Dean was a probie at the time, new to rangering and rescue. "It was awful," he told me. "I called Bob, who was duty officer, and told him I needed help right away, but he took his time coming."

Dean saw a package of hot dogs and quickly deduced what had happened. He turned the child over, whacked the back, and expelled a chunk of frankfurter like a shot from the toddler's throat.

He always seemed to be around when these things happened. Plus, when we started working together, he was diabetic and pushing retirement age and had suffered every ailment known to medicine and some unknown ones, too.

So I was nervous when he moved into Kidney.

What I got was a lot of fun, an education, and more meals than I could count. I think Dean helped me with my own injuries more than I ever had to help with his, and when he landed at Stream Camp, the ranger housing at Kidney, he seemed to dispel whatever curse had hung over his early days. It was like he was meant to be there.

A master fisherman, Dean had been combing these woods since he was a kid in the '50s. He remembered a pat on the head from Governor Baxter himself one day when his family was picnicking at Avalanche Field. He knew the ins and outs of every pond in the woods north of Millinocket and which fly to use where and when, and unlike most anglers, he was happy to share his secrets. He even loaned out his private canoe to many campers.

He liked nothing better than telling stories, and he was ever quick with one-liners. We'd be finishing a roof and he'd pound the final nail in the cap, then sit back and say, "Good enough for the girls I go with," or "Beautiful, just like the girl I married." On the rare occasion when a piece of trim didn't quite line up right or a corner was a hair off level, he'd scratch his beard and say, "Can't see it from my camp." If I was considering making some adjustments to fix such an issue, he'd tell me, "If we did it any better, they wouldn't believe we did it."

He was fearless and became the shop steward of our union, much to the chagrin of HQ. I remember cracking up when he told our previous chief, "You're no ranger. You live in a town and work in an office." The normal repercussions for insubordinate talk didn't faze him.

On another occasion we were cutting firewood together at the Togue service area, a huge parking and equipment lot at the south end of the park, where the Scientific Forest Management Area would drop tree-length wood to be readied for the various campgrounds. Several rangers were sawing and working the splitter. The same chief showed up as we were packing it in for the day. "Oh, here he is," said Dean. "Just like a blister. Shows up when the work's done."

As we finished whichever project we were working on, Dean would walk toward his truck and then turn and say, "Coming for supper?" And I usually did. He shot or caught almost all of the protein that graced the table, and both he and Charity knew what to do with it. During the decade we worked together, I dined at Stream Camp, tucked in the woods by the Nesowadnehunk, more often than I ate at my own camp. There would usually be several of us around the table, with a couple of park handhelds on the refrigerator, eating venison burgers or moose stew or other delicious entrees more organic than anything at Whole Foods. We'd talk park politics, trade tales about campers, or listen to Dean recount one of his fishing adventures for the hour and a half we had for our dinner.

Then it was back to duty stations in the dark.

————

It wasn't Dean we rescued during those years but Charity. Dean and I had a regular Laurel and Hardy routine when it came to her: "She's my partner," I'd say with a smile in Charity's direction.

"She's my *wife*," he'd respond.

"Yes, but she's *my* partner."

One August day, Charity and my supervisor, Jodi, a tall 50-something redhead from Grand Rapids, Minnesota, had us working on the woodpile at Foster Field despite the fact that it was in the low 90s and humid. "We'll only be a few hours and drink plenty of water," Jodi said, admitting that even her boss didn't think it was a good idea. Drink water we did, as Charity ran the wood splitter and I bucked up the tree-length timbers on the pile. Dressed in chaps and a helmet, raining down sweat, I frequently gestured for Charity to drink, making the universal frat boy "bottoms up" salute. I'd look over and she'd be paused, motioning the same to me.

We made a small dent in the 8-foot wall of boles and bark, readying firewood for the sheds in our respective campgrounds. This was the stuff that would keep our campers warm at the end of fall, through the deep of winter, and into the late spring, when temperatures could still dip into the 40s. The heavy work was certainly warming *us* that day.

At lunch, Charity, her face flushed, hopped into her truck for the short ride back to her camp.

She didn't make it.

Only a short while later, Bruce came flying up, his flashers going. He stopped, shouted what sounded like "heatstroke, extreme case," to me in my ear protection, and gunned it north up the road.

"What'd he say?" I asked Jodi.

"Heatstroke, Stream Camp," she said, making for her truck.

We sped off in that direction and found Charity slumped on the ground next to the open door of her pickup, twitching, as if she'd collapsed upon stepping out. Bruce was leaning over her, and Dean was pacing, frantic.

"Get any ice you can find," Bruce said. Jodi and I ran to the freezer in Dean and Charity's small camp. Luckily, they had some venison sausage and other frozen meats. We poured bottles of water over Charity's head, put the icy foil-wrapped packages under her armpits and behind her neck, and fanned her.

She just lay there, barely breathing.

Dean was out of his mind with worry and kept getting in the way. Jodi took him off to the side to keep him from slowing us down.

Nothing we did worked. She seemed comatose.

"Let's get her in the shower," said Bruce. He and I got on either side of Charity, and Jodi opened doors. We shuffled her into the small fiberglass shower stall off the bedroom, sat her on a chair, and turned on cold water. This had the effect we were looking for: Charity began to come to, mumbling, in a haze. She didn't know how she'd gotten there or what happened. We trained the cooling blast on her for several minutes. Then we stepped out as Jodi wrapped her in a towel.

"I'm going to take her to the hospital," the boss told us. "I think she's going to be fine, but she should get checked out." We all agreed this was wise and helped slide Charity onto the bench seat in Jodi's truck. They hightailed it to Millinocket.

We found out later that Charity had no recollection of driving back to Stream Camp. The Millinocket doctor diagnosed her with heat syncope, an illness that falls somewhere between dangerous heatstroke and harmless fainting. When the already-overheated ranger got into her truck, said the doc, it was like she stepped into a blast furnace. Her body compensated by dilating her vessels in an effort to cool her skin, which had the effect of shutting down blood flow to the brain, causing her to pass out. Dean also seemed about ready to collapse.

That would happen down the road a few years.

Word is flowing from one duty station to the next that another full-time position has opened. One of the new year-rounders has given his notice, due to a family issue. Because we live in the park and get mail infrequently, we typically hear park news through our truck windows, stopping on the road to chat when we see other vehicles with the Baxter Park decal on the door.

When I hired on at the park full time, vacancies were unheard of. These jobs were coveted, and people held them for decades. I started at Baxter just as the era of ranger cowboys was ending. I feel lucky that I got to know Bob Howes and Loren Goode and Barry MacArthur, who came up together, starting at the park in the '6os. I learned a lot from all of them, but I learned the most from Bob, who was my supervisor for years.

"You putting in for the law enforcement position?" Bruce asks. He already knows the answer.

My wife didn't grow up wanting to be a park ranger, and while she's patient and helpful and has allowed me to pursue this work, the travel and time apart wears on her. Really wears on her. Uprooting the family—we often mention how fortunate we are for our house, our neighborhood, and our school district—just wouldn't work at this point, which makes applying for a position at the next level impossible.

In some ways, though, I prefer the work of a seasonal. Aside from Bruce, who has a camp near Abol Beach in the south end of the park, none of the other rangers live here full time, and to me, park rangers should live in parks. I want to hear the far-off murmur of the falls, the yapping of coyotes, and the moans of moose as I fall asleep. That's part of the point of being here.

My wife has always loved the place, and has done her best to support me, but it isn't easy. She's a beach person and wishes we could do more together during what she considers the best part of the year. I'm a mountain guy. She's from the suburbs, I'm from the woods. We were mismatched from the day we met at Clark University, but with the attraction of opposites, we came together.

Being away for three and a half days a week for six months is difficult for all of us, and it's made even more difficult by the fact that I spend a lot of time when I'm home from the park working on my other job to help pay for my lifestyle. The way I look at it, I don't see my people for three days a week during my 26 weeks in the park. Now, two and a half months is a long time, but my brother-in-law, a colonel in the U.S. Army Reserves, deployed to Iraq for two years. (I always like to quote him the old Army Ranger maxim, "Rangers lead the way." And he always replies, "Not your kind of ranger.")

My duty doesn't actually take me away from my family for 78 days when you factor in vacation and the numerous visits they make to Daicey Pond. Add all that up, and I go absentee about 50 days of Leo's life each year. Which is still a lot, and I get that. I miss some school events, and I can't attend any of his travel-team soccer matches because they're on Sundays.

But because of this job, I'm home six months straight, plus those three days a week, all day every day. I pick Leo up from school, play soccer in the yard, read to him at night. All tallied, I bet I spend more focused time with him than do most dads with their children.

And in return for my absence, he and Gus have grown up in a genuine wilderness, away from video games, learning how to improvise and how to use tools, meeting people from around the globe, having adventures. Among the other rangers, Leo is known as "the football," a nickname born of an all-night rescue I did, during which he was passed from one ranger to the next while I was on the mountain. He loves to explore, play cards with me during my evening office hours, cook s'mores, and get together with the daughter of another ranger for epic games of Monopoly.

My older son, Gus, was the same way, going with me to work and helping me on countless projects during his time at the park, calling himself the "senior of the junior rangers." When he was small, he liked to rake sites. "Everyone gets a Zen garden," I'd tell him, and he thought that was great. He'd dutifully start making intricate designs in the dirt around the firepit, doing his part to help campers relax. As he grew, he held the level while I installed stairs, drilled the holes for the new water bars, painted cabins, and demolished the old bridge at Katahdin Stream Falls, among a zillion other things. He even rescued some stranded girls once, paddling out and retrieving their boats, which had drifted off when they hopped onto a rock in the middle of the pond.

He always loved coming with me, spending the whole shift. Charity routed his name on a brown wooden sign that hung beneath mine, listing rangers on duty, and he inherited a mini ranger uniform, complete with badge and name tag, from older park kids. He'd run up when I was working on something to tell me he was going hiking with the Hewetts or climbing with the Jumps or that he was heading down to Cabin 1 to play chess with the Wickards. I'd save hiking projects for his visits, and we'd march off to cut blowdowns, talking about soccer superstars or characters from the books we read together. He'd paddle around the pond, exploring. Rangers would come by and take him fishing as he grew. Sometimes he'd get a little stir-crazy when no one else was around, but he called it "good bored."

My wife sees the value in all this, which is one of the reasons I'm still here. I'm proud to share this place with my boys and with campers from all around the world. And she also understands that it's important work. Not just to me but to the wider world. While my sister's husband is an actual warrior, I like to think of myself as a foot soldier for wild places, preserving and defending one of the last great natural bastions in the East.

I've seen the park work its enchantments countless times—relaxing the uptight, bonding families, wowing young kids, spreading awe among adults—and I'm a firm believer the world needs wildlands to remind us what it means to be human.

CHAPTER 13

A CAR COMES FLYING INTO THE PARKING LOT, TRAILING CLOUDS OF dust. I step out of the ranger station and recognize the blue Subaru belonging to the two 30-something sisters from the Bath area staying in Cabin 4. One of the women jumps out of the car and bolts toward me. I wait for her to start screaming.

Bruce has a thing about people sprinting through public areas in Baxter Park. "There's no running in the campground," he always tells them good-naturedly. Running is almost always bad, according to his way of thinking, and not because he's worried about someone tripping on the park's famous collection of rocks and roots or making us old paunchy guys feel older and paunchier.

Many of our rescues begin with someone dashing frantically toward a duty station. Runners ruin hot meals. They put an end to evening fishing trips. They terminate our rare ranger cookouts. They kill a night with a good book. They prevent us from going off duty. It's happened innumerable times. Nothing says distress like a sprinting camper.

So, just like at the pool, no running, please.

I remember one particular situation almost identical to this one. On that sunny summer morning, in my second season, another speeding Japanese import came careening to a stop in roughly the same spot, depositing a distraught young lady into the parking lot. I saw it all happen from my desk, where I was taking down the day's weather and munching on a

Pop Tart. The girl, high school or early college age, ran toward the station screaming, "She can't breathe, she's going to die!"

Still a probie, I had a bit of a palpitation with this talk of death, and the look of her didn't help. Her hair was a bird's nest, her eyes were wide, and her hiking tights, T-shirt, and face—her entire body all the way up to her ponytail—were covered in dried blood. She looked like the hiking equivalent of Stephen King's Carrie at the prom. She stood there staring at me, gasping.

I took a couple of deep breaths myself and then managed to quietly say, "Slow down. Easy. Who can't breathe?"

As she composed herself, I realized the substance caked to her was not gore. It was plain old Baxter mud, which settled my nerves a bit. She was a summer camp counselor and had tumbled her way down Mount OJI, running to get help for one of her campers, who was having trouble breathing about a mile up the peak.

My first thought was: bee sting. At the time, we did not carry epinephrine in our rescue packs. If no one in her party had an EpiPen, we might already be too late.

I stopped at Cabin 5 on the way to my truck, recruiting a physician's assistant I knew was staying there. When I had checked her in the previous day, she'd offered to help if I had any issues. She joined me in the cab, the counselor jumped in the bed, and I radioed it in. We spun tires on our way to the trailhead a couple of miles away.

We made good time on the bogs and ledges of OJI and arrived to find a group of middle schoolers. Some were pacing. Others were crying. Among them was a ponytailed 13-year-old, sitting on a rock with her knees up, gasping for air. Her skin was pale, her eyes frantic, and she was shaking. A counselor came over and told us the girl was complaining of chest pain. Blurred vision. Dizziness. Numbness in arms and legs.

I knelt down, told her I was a ranger and there to help, and introduced her to the PA, who began an examination while I asked questions. Allergies? No. Asthma? No. What had she had to eat? Granola cereal for breakfast. A protein bar for a snack. Plenty to drink.

"Get me a paper bag," said the PA. I asked around, and a girl offered her snack sack. The PA had her breathe into it.

Turned out the teen was having a panic attack, nothing more. No bee sting. She was never at risk of dying. It was an early lesson for me: an emergency might not be as serious as it's made out to be by the reporting party. This mud-covered camp counselor had medical training equal to my own, and she panicked as much as the young girl when all the moment called for was a bit of calm. I filed this away.

Once the young girl relaxed, I talked to the group leaders about what might have caused this situation. "Not sure," one said. "We got here the other day and did South Turner. Then we hiked up to Chimney Pond. Yesterday we climbed Katahdin, and today we thought we'd climb OJI." I pointed out that scaling all these peaks was an extremely ambitious itinerary for a bunch of middle schoolers, and it was obviously too much for this young camper.

"What about a paddling day?" I suggested. "Or maybe a swim or a splash-around at Ledge Falls." They agreed this made sense.

A few days later the chief stopped by. A gray-haired character soon to retire, he was famous for his thigh-slapping stories and for always wearing a hard hat coated in grease to collect the bugs. He smiled and said, "You sounded nervous on the radio, were you nervous?"

I explained that, yeah, I was nervous. A woman who appeared to be covered in blood had come into my campground screaming, "She's going to die." I thought it was a bee sting and I would find a dead young camper.

I could tell by the look on his face that I failed some sort of test. Real rangers, apparently, don't get spooked.

On this morning, I wait in front of the ranger station for the woman from Bath to call out for help. But she zips past me up the trail to her cabin. Seconds later, she reappears, canters to the blue car, and peels out of the lot.

An hour later, I'm in the day-use parking area picking up trash when the same Subaru speeds through on the way back. The other sister is driving. I hold up my hand for her to stop. She does so and powers down her window, looking down at her lap.

"Going kinda fast," I say. "It's fifteen through here. You need to watch the speed."

She apologizes and then beams at me, her eyes lighting up behind her tortoiseshell frames. "We just saw a moose."

"Yeah, I know," I said.

She tilts her head back and looks intently at me. "You know?"

"Well, you sped up into the campground but weren't looking for help. Usually people moving that fast—outside of emergency situations—are getting either their cameras or a friend to show them the charismatic megafauna."

She nods. "A cow and a calf, nursing in the road." There's a touch of awe in her voice.

"I hope you gave mama her space, especially with a calf in tow," I said.

"Oh, we did," she assures me.

I've seen moose many times in Maynard's Marsh, the bog that sits astride Daicey Pond Road about halfway to the campground. This verdant pool has everything they want—water, water grasses, more water grasses—and some things they don't seem to care much about, such as a pull-the-car-over view of Katahdin, with all its neighboring, skyscraping peaks. The moose were probably in the water for most of the time, and my speed racer likely couldn't have gotten too close without getting wet. All aglow, she heads up the road into the campground.

She's one of the lucky ones. Moose have been scarce in recent years, at least compared with when I started out. Climate change seems to be taking its toll on the largest member of the deer family. Our family always saw moose when we vacationed at the park. (When we didn't, my mom used to have my dad pull over, and we kids would pile out, pretend we saw one, and point at a pond, just to see how many people we could get to stop.)

During my first few seasons, I'd spot the big brown beasts at least once a shift. They'd be standing in the road on my drive in, munching the sopping greenery at Stump Pond, or hanging at the marshes along the Daicey and Kidney roads. I'd bump into them while hiking alongside Nesowadnehunk Stream or when checking on canoes at Grassy Pond. At the very least, I'd see sign. A hoofprint here. A pile of "bonbons" there. They were always around.

For the past decade, though, moose seemed to have mostly disappeared. I may spy one a month these days. The difference in ten years is dramatic.

Wildlife biologists have confirmed the decline, one of the many consequences of a changing climate. Warming temperatures have welcomed the winter tick into northern Maine, and these tiny parasites have arrived in such numbers that they're wreaking havoc on the Pine Tree State's celebrity furbearers. The clustering arachnids have killed thousands of moose in just a few years.

Known for spreading in big clouds, winter ticks can bring down an adult, but they are especially deadly to calves, overwhelming them with sheer numbers. Researcher Peter Pekins, who's studied the phenomenon in Maine and New Hampshire, told the *New York Times* that the average number of ticks he's counted per animal is 47,000, but some have had twice that many. At Baxter Park, we've found dead moose on trails in the spring with huge growths comprised of these tiny vampires. The good news: the winter tick is not a threat to humans—it's very happy with moose, thanks—and it's the only tick we see in any sort of numbers in the park.

There may be other reasons why the moose population is declining within Baxter. Some rangers conjecture it's because all the land around the park is now in conservation and, ironically, moose seem to like cut-over paper company lands, which brim with tasty fresh growth. Other rangers think maybe moose are moving north to avoid the temps and the ticks. Whatever the reason, the population is not what it used to be.

But they're not gone yet. In fact, this year seems to be a relatively good one. We had several in or around Daicey Pond, including this cow and calf, which wandered through the campground on multiple occasions. I've already laid eyes on more than have become typical in recent seasons, and park visitors, like the sisters from Bath, appreciate the fact that they're around.

Many campers like them a little *too* much. Moose need elbow room—they're pretty much all elbows to begin with—and a lot of park visitors don't seem to get this. Most people see them as docile, dumb, and harmless, but they could do some serious damage simply due to their size. Moose can weigh more than a half ton and they could *trip* and kill you. And they always seem ready to stumble, so ungainly are they on their overly long legs. If a moose took a step backward and didn't notice you there, it could easily break your foot, cave in your skull, or make a divot in your chest.

Nobody worries about that though. But, now that I think about it, there was one pair of 20-something Francophones from Montreal who cowered in their cabin one summer night in fear of a moose. The two women were in Cabin 1, the all-window, waterside gem that the regulars compete for; they had lucked into a single-night stay thanks to the vagaries of internet booking. Lovely ladies, they were newbies, of the kind that one ranger says would do better staying on the tarmac. I was standing by the pond when they appeared in the morning with bad cases of bed head and told me they got no sleep.

"How come?" I asked. "Mattress not comfortable?" Our mattresses are surprisingly comfy.

"No. A moose was trying to get into our cabin."

"Really?" I said. "What makes you think that?"

"It was grunting right outside."

"Grunting?"

This surprised me. Moose make a lot of noise during rutting season, in late September and October, but are usually not heard much around the campground in June. I asked the women to make the noise for me. They both gave me a deep, unmistakable, batrachian croak. Amphibious even.

"You sure it was a moose?"

"Well . . . " said one. "We were pretty sure. It sounded like it was right out in front of our cabin, and we huddled together in the corner."

"I think it *was* right out in front of your cabin—"

"We also heard wolves," the other one interrupted. Then she looked at me sheepishly, pushing a strand of hair behind her ear.

I hadn't heard about marauding moose or prowling wolves from any of the residents of the other nine cabins.

"Really?" I said. "What did *they* sound like?"

"Well, it almost sounded like they were out on the pond. They went..."

She proceeded to yodel, making an ululating sound that was also instantly recognizable.

I explained to the pair that the two fearsome critters that had them cowering in their cabin were in fact bullfrogs and loons, which, while they can sound creepy at night, don't usually pose much of a threat. I told the women I didn't think a moose could actually get up on the porch—the stairs are too narrow for their wide-spread legs, and its rack wouldn't fit under the roof line. A moose certainly wouldn't know how to use a door handle.

"A frog and a bird?" one said, incredulous.

"Frog and a bird," I replied. "And be careful, because they're still out there."

Put a bunch of people with little woodland experience into a forest playground, and these sorts of interactions become commonplace. In the past five years, I've probably had a half dozen campers confuse loons with wolves. Neither the park nor the state is home to any wolves, although one of the most skeptical, no-BS rangers I've worked with told me he was sure he had seen one standing in the road at the top of Abol Hill. People talk of seeing them in this or that corner of Maine. But, officially, no wolves have lived in Maine since the late nineteenth or early twentieth century.

We do have a thriving population of coyotes, however. We had a coyote family living between Daicey and Kidney a couple of years ago with three pups that were routinely spotted over in Kidney's big field. One loped along the road beside my truck once, a tiny little fellow, clearly the runt, and I was tempted to stop and open the passenger door to let him hop up onto the seat beside me because he seemed that habituated to people. Of course, I didn't. I just watched him trot for probably a quarter mile before he looked back at me and stepped off into the woods.

I often fall asleep at night to the sound of that pup and his siblings and all their cousins yipping and barking on the other side of the stream, another nice reminder of how wild these woods remain.

———————

The moose and her calf reminded me of another popular wildland baby in Baxter Park, arguably the best-known creature on the globe, adored from America to Asia, Alaska to Australia. More renowned, in fact, than even Governor Baxter himself. This young deer, with his expressive brown eyes and fluffy white tail, is a matinee idol, adorning T-shirts, smiling down from posters, and inspiring stuffed toys and an empire of animated films. His father was the Great Prince of the Forest, we all worried when his mother was taken by a hunter, and his story exemplified man's domineering attitude toward nature. The tiny guy helped influence generations of conservationists.

Bambi, you see, is one of ours: a Baxter Park denizen. When Walt Disney was making the 1942 blockbuster, he was planning to use a mule deer from Arrowhead, California, as the model for its protagonist. One of his illustrators objected, insisting that the big-eared deer common to the West looked nothing like the European roe deer from the book by Felix Salten. Bambi, the illustrator said, should be a white-tailed deer from his home state of Maine. Disney told him to go find him a deer.

That illustrator, Maurice "Jake" Day, a native of Damariscotta, Maine, knew just where to look. An artist whose work had appeared in *Life*, *Atlantic Monthly*, *Vanity Fair*, and *Outdoor Life*, Day was also an avid outdoor explorer, and his exploits were famously described in the works of his friend Edmund Ware Smith, a *Field & Stream* author. For this task, Day returned to his hometown, gathered his camera and a buddy, and made for the woods around Katahdin.

Disney gave him a list of items he wanted to show in the film, including birch trees, blueberry bushes, marsh grass, pinecones, and hazelnuts, and

Day spent several months taking thousands of photographs and drawing a range of sketches of the park's pristine forest. At night he and his friend Lester Hall sat in their tent reading the script and thinking about locations; by day they went out looking for just the right fawn. In all that time, they had difficulty finding the ideal setting for the story until they ventured into what is now the center of the park, near Russell Pond.

Day's work at Baxter sold Walt Disney, who decided the movie should take place in a forest like this one and Bambi should be a white-tailed fawn. The Maine Department of Economic Development arranged to have two 4-month-old orphaned deer shipped to California to serve as models for studio animators. Day's illustrations inspired the backdrops. When the film was released, Walt Disney wanted the premiere to be in Augusta, Maine, as a thank-you to Jake, but state officials objected due to fears of pushback from Maine's large pro-hunting community. Instead, *Bambi* opened in London and then in New York City.

In 1967, Governor Baxter appointed Maurice "Jake" Day the park's official artist in residence. The famed illustrator continued to visit Baxter Park with an assemblage of friends—including the Supreme Court's longest-serving justice, William O. Douglas—who collectively became known as "Jake's Rangers." On his trips to the park, Day produced many paintings of Katahdin and its lieutenants. He climbed the mountain on his 75th birthday and planned to do so again on his 80th, but the early July blackflies reportedly drove him off. Jake Day's drawing of a mountain and a moose became the official park seal and still features on the doors of our trucks.

———————

The Quebecois ladies who were creeped out by a bullfrog and a loon were far from the only city folks to be unnerved by the park's woodland creatures. Several seasons back we had a Daicey Pond visitor that induced mental breakdowns in almost every rental cabin. Cute little guest, roughly 8 inches tall and covered in fuzzy fluff. Brown and rust colored with two great big, friendly eyes, he was the sort of Baxter denizen that sells postcards. He was docile and peaceful and nestled into an evergreen somewhere just off the Appalachian Trail.

The campers wanted to wring his fragile neck.

Northern saw-whet owls are widespread across the North Woods, nesting in dark cavities. This typically means hollowed-out old trees, which are common throughout Baxter Park. Like most owls, they're nocturnal, and they're a fairly secretive species, rarely seen.

But—and here's where the issue with my campers lay—they're occasionally heard. This little fellow moved in near Kidney Pond one week, driving the campers there to distraction with his call. Then he relocated to a tree up near Cabin 10 at Daicey.

It sounded like a dump truck was in reverse in the woods between the campground and the Appalachian Trail. All. Night. Long. This saw-whet was looking for company, not at all like Friend Owl in *Bambi*, who was fed up with the springtime ritual. The little lothario cried out, loud enough to echo off the pond, two or three times a second, for hours on end. *Beep, beep, beep.* He repeated his appeal about 100 times a minute, from dusk to dawn. This owl was apparently very, very lonely. Eight inches tall with a voice as big as the pond.

On a few occasions he would tease campers by going quiet for a moment, perhaps making himself more comfortable on his branch, and you could almost feel the tension dissipate, as if everyone joined in a collective sigh. Then he'd start up again. He usually decided at about 4 A.M. that he wasn't going to find anyone to go home with and went to sleep. Night after night after night.

The campers slept later than usual that week and they staggered out of their cabins in the morning with intent to kill. It's a good thing none of them could find this little guy.

Being a nature preserve, Baxter Park abounds with sounds. Everyone's favorite (with the exception of two ladies from Montreal) is probably the loon. Then maybe the spring peepers. Bullfrogs harrumph on the shore of Daicey like a Greek chorus (or a carousing moose). A regular visitor who runs a liquor store in Providence comes every year just to listen to the frog chorale. One year she came to my office in tears because they were too quiet and it ruined her vacation.

We have woodpeckers that laugh maniacally and lots of chattering fliers, like grackles and red-winged blackbirds. We have tittering squirrels and moaning little minks. On lucky days we get to hear the flutelike trill of the hermit thrush, the *old Sam Peabody, Peabody, Peabody* of the white-throated sparrow, and the hoot of a barred owl. I've been screamed at by a bobcat, which sounds like someone being stabbed in a horror movie; growled at by a fox kit, which was more amusing than menacing; and blown at by a black bear, who didn't like being shooed away from the snack-filled backpacks of nervous AT hikers at the Birches.

This was my only experience with a saw-whet, however. Bruce once had to free one that got stuck in an outhouse—down in the vault with all the good stuff—but I missed that particular rescue.

By the end of my week, the talkative little fella had moved far enough away that he was no longer bothersome, now sounding like a distant police siren.

"What was that beeping I heard all week?" a camper asked me as he packed his car to leave. I told him.

"Impressive," he said, with the respect of someone well-beaten by a worthy adversary.

I nodded in agreement.

"A little owl?" he said, again turning to look at me.

I nodded.

"Impressive," he repeated.

I had just barely heard the saw-whet's entreaties at my cabin. It wasn't the owl that kept me up, it was the coyotes that howled and screeched like a coven of witches on the far side of the stream. I'm sure no one in the campground heard them over the saw-whet, but they were close enough to my cabin to startle me awake.

And then the mosquitoes started.

Moose can get ornery on occasion. They have a violent side, but they usually turn it toward their own kind in an awesome spectacle I hope to witness in person someday. Campers have shown me cell phone videos of two bulls locking horns over a female down by the stream, and a couple of years ago, we had a pair fight to the death up at Trout Brook Crossing. In that case, someone noticed a dead bull lying underneath the bridge, which sits 15 feet above the brook. A little investigation led the rangers up north to believe that one moose essentially forced the other off the bridge, and it broke its neck in the fall.

Females with young can also turn from photogenic to enraged in a second. I know at least a couple of rangers chased by angry mamas, including one who ran all through Abol Campground trying to get away. (Not sure what she would have done had she caught him.)

I had my own run-in with a moose once, at about midnight, down in the same area. I was driving in on a Friday, which is typically what I do to be ready for my shift on Saturday morning. This keeps a ranger in the campground overnight—Charity often heads out after going off at 9— and gets me a lot more sleep than waking up at 3 A.M. in Appleton to be on duty at 7 at Daicey.

When I got to Abol Hill on that September evening years ago, I came upon a yearling in the middle of the road. These juveniles can often be found trotting along the park thoroughfare, having been chased off by their mothers with the arrival of new calves. Like human teenagers, they're pretty confused about what to do with their lives at this point and tend to make some bad decisions. It's not uncommon to drive behind one for miles before it has the sense to leave the road.

In this case, I did what I always do: pulled over and sat and let him have his space as he jogged along ahead. When I got back on my way five minutes later, I caught up to him and stopped again, trying to be as respectful as possible but also wanting to get to my camp and go to sleep. We did this dance for miles, passing dozens of openings where he could have comfortably stepped into the woods. (Snowshoe hares are much the same, refusing to yield the road, frantically darting this way and that.)

We were almost at the Grassy/Tracy parking lot when he decided he'd had enough.

I came around a corner and found him atop a small rise, head down, ready to charge. (Moose don't like headlights, for one.) I stopped, giving him plenty of room, and waited to see what would happen. He barreled right down the road at me, all flaring nostrils, wide eyes, and 5-inch hooves. My eyes got wide, too, and I slammed my little diesel VW in reverse, going backward as fast as I could, navigating with my side mirrors so I could keep my main focus on the moose. I eventually bumped into the road bank, the little foot-high wall of roots and rocks that lines the Park Tote Road in places, and came to a stop. I couldn't go back any farther.

He kept coming.

The moose ran straight at me and then swerved, going up the bank between my car and the woods before falling over right beside my passenger door. I panicked a moment, worrying that I had somehow hit him, but then remembered that I wasn't moving. He leaned on my hood to stand, denting the trim up near the windshield, and then climbed back into the road, turning to give me one last look, as if to say, "We done?" Then he zipped off into the black woods as if nothing had ever happened.

My heart told me otherwise.

CHAPTER 14

Somehow, people are much more frightened of bears than of moose, which outweigh bears by three times and have built-in spikes on their heads expressly designed for intimidation. Somehow, they are cute and bears are scary. When campers grill me about our ursine population (and they do), I usually tell them that they'll have far more to worry about with blackflies and mosquitoes. As far as I know, there's never been a bear attack in Baxter State Park. There hasn't been a fatal wild bear encounter in *Maine* since a century before the founding of the park. This is likely due to the fact that we have an abundant natural food supply for bears, and rangers actively police people and their garbage. At this point, even the mice in the park are more problematic. (I had to brain one earlier this season as it scurried about my bedroom at 3 A.M.) Insects and arachnids most definitely harm and kill more people each year than any other animals found in the park.

But bears are undoubtedly the bogeybeasts of the backcountry, at least based on the questions of nervous campers.

Most park visitors never see a bruin, let alone have a negative encounter. I've come across a dozen or so in 18 years at Baxter Park, and the majority were flashing their asses at me as they ran off into the woods. Only a couple have lingered for any length of time, and both of these were harmless, more curious than anything else. I spotted a good-sized specimen crossing the road at South Branch Pond early this season. Russ

Porter told me later that the bear stuck around all summer, just enjoying the campground like everyone else.

"He'd sit there in the road flipping rocks over and eating grubs but wouldn't bother anybody," he said. "Minding his own business. People spotted him all kinds of times."

For some reason we don't seem to have the Yogi types at Baxter. We have thousands of black bears roaming our woods, but very few of the super-clever variety that you hear about at parks out West, unscrewing the tops off containers and picking locks. We did have an apocryphal "Toll Bear" on the trail to Slaughter Pond years ago, who sat in the trail and didn't allow anglers to pass until presented with a trout. We had another clever fellow at one time that apparently recognized people had few options when hiking on the Knife Edge and sat expectantly waiting for treats. Unfortunately, he got them, which only attracts bears to more negative encounters. The park naturalist was worried that *climbers* would scare the *bear*, and it would get hurt trying to run away.

Not that they don't do some damage here. Bears big and little have climbed onto and into cars, tearing up the upholstery. They've stuck their paws into cracked windows and shattered the glass. One even slashed the screen and crawled onto the porch at my old camp. (A drunk human also once cut through a screen and climbed into my camp, which I find more disturbing.)

We've had a couple of bears claw holes in the sides of tents with people inside, attracted by the scent of strawberry shampoo, but no one was hurt. At Daicey Pond, I can recall only one real problem bear, and it visited when I was off duty. Charity told me later that it ambled up onto the picnic table at Cabin 7 while the occupants were dutifully putting away food after making breakfast. They were doing everything right, locking away tempting bear treats in their car, except that they left their pancakes on the table as they did so. The bear liked these flapjacks very much. Mayhem ensued when the couple returned to find their uninvited guest. Charity heard the ruckus and alerted the duty officer, who arrived with bear spray and loud music in an effort to drive the animal off. Some bears apparently don't mind bear spray and high-volume hits, including this particular one. As with obnoxious drunks, it took some doing to solve the problem. The bear eventually wandered off, bored.

When we do find bruins causing issues, we treat them the same way we do other troublemakers: we ask them to leave the park. Usually this involves a bunch of bacon and garbage and a big old culvert converted into an ursid paddy wagon.

For all that, I've never rescued anyone for a problem arising from our most-feared population, but I have been covered in a patient's blood, readying her for the emergency room, as a result of the North Woods' most vicious resident: the blackfly.

These tiny insects share the tick's fondness for human blood. The females do, anyway. The males live off nectar. Across the globe, there are more than 2,200 varieties of blackflies, and they have been known to transmit disease in Africa and South America. In Baxter Park, they transmit little itchy welts.

The issue with blackflies, of course, is the sheer numbers. We have millions in Maine, typically between Mother's Day and Father's Day, according to the old saw. In Baxter there is no season. The eating is good, and they don't appear to want to leave after the holidays. They arrive shortly after we do in the spring and pester us into early summer, returning in the fall for Labor Day, "wearing overcoats," as one old ranger used to say.

The little bastards particularly seem to enjoy visiting when I'm dressed in chain saw gear or when I'm painting. In other words, when I'm standing still and don't have hands to defend myself. On more than one occasion, I've had to flee indoors to maintain my sanity.

When I started at the park, I was sent to chain saw training in the north end during high blackfly season. As a probie, I assumed all of the rangers would be too macho to be bothered by these pinhead-size vampires. I was really surprised to find a bunch of guys sitting around in head nets and whole-body mesh insect suits, pragmatism trumping machismo. Campers always ask what we use for repellent, and the answer, for me, is nothing. I haven't found any product that works for any length of time. Our old chief used to slather his ever-present hard hat with grease, and it would be covered by the end of the day, a grisly field of bodies, but he still had to slap others.

In July, we get the whole demonic trifecta: blackflies, mosquitoes, and horseflies. Charity calls the latter "Andyflies" because these members of *Tabanidae* seem to love me. When we were spending long summer days working on the camp we now live in, in teams of five or six rangers, the biting flies always found me, making maddening orbits around my head by the dozen.

When Leo and I were driving through the park on our way home late in July this year we ended up behind a black Suburban, at least twenty horseflies aswirl behind the vehicle, as if riding its draft. These bugs are not waiting for the car to pull over and the occupants to exit—though they'll happily take advantage of that—but are attracted to dark, moving objects, especially shiny ones. At Togue Gate, they merged with the great fog of blackflies and mosquitoes that haunt that marshy locale.

When all three of these bloodsuckers appear, they're enough to make one question one's childhood dream of being a park ranger.

––––––––––

I learned just how vicious blackflies can be on an on-duty hike of the Traveler Loop, a 10-mile circuit up and over Traveler and North Traveler mountains and Peak of the Ridges that rivals Katahdin for difficulty. The trail had been open for a couple of years, and I had never had a chance to sample it, so my supervisor scheduled a day that I could do so. Another ranger covered my campground, and I drove the truck north at about 5:30 A.M., the light just breaking over the trees, taking advantage of some nice June weather. Little did I know that this was a major mistake.

I like nothing better than getting paid to hike, and I left South Branch Pond Campground early, taking in the views as the trail slides along the pond and climbs the side of Center Ridge. We recommend that hikers follow the route counterclockwise, scaling Peak of the Ridges in the morning and descending North Traveler in the afternoon. This eases them into the hike and deposits them almost back in the campground at the end of the day, so that was my plan.

I had made it about halfway around the circuit when I came upon them. Two bodies lying at the side of the trail, back to a tree, wrapped in plastic. The scene looked like a gangland hit from the movies, when the victim gets rolled up in a shower curtain to be dumped somewhere. I looked around for a Soprano.

I hadn't heard of anyone missing. We occasionally receive APBs from the law enforcement community, but I wasn't aware of one. I stood for a moment and took in the scene, catching my breath. I couldn't see any blood or signs of trauma. The area around the pair, a little mixed wood vale, didn't appear unusual or disturbed in any way. I wondered how anyone could have dropped two bodies here—a plane seemed unlikely, given their clearly arranged position—and knelt to take a closer look.

I jumped back when one of the plastic-wrapped figures opened its eyes with a start. We stared at each other, shocked.

Hands appeared and undid the head covering, revealing the pleasant face of a woman about my age. She began to talk rapidly at me in French. "Parlez vous?" she asked when I showed no signs of comprehension. The other "body" came alive with the commotion and began to peel off layers, too. Another woman, this one slightly older.

"Uh, no," I replied.

They both smiled with relief to see my ranger uniform. The younger woman, Claudette, with a tangle of brown hair and big brown eyes, like a model who'd let herself go in retirement, could speak halting English. She told me she and her friend, Monique, were from Montreal and were camping at South Branch. They'd gone for a hike the previous day and gotten lost because they didn't understand the signage. They'd spent the night in the woods and were out of food and water. The plastic mummification was to protect themselves from the incessant blackflies.

I fished out the snacks I had in my bag and offered them some peanut butter crackers and energy bars, which they accepted thankfully. I gave them each a water bottle and thought to myself that it would be a long hike if I was the only one with any supplies.

I looked at my watch and realized that while the rangers at South Branch hadn't been looking for missing hikers when I spoke to them that morning, they would wonder what was up when these women didn't leave their site at 11, checkout time. I stepped away and made a call. I could only reach Russell Pond, due to the fickleness of radio waves, but I let the ranger there know that I had found two lost overnight hikers and would be escorting them around Traveler Loop.

We spent the rest of the day painstakingly making our way back toward South Branch Pond. On a normal hike it would be a spectacular trail, with long ridge walks, views of the surrounding mountains, and lots of lovely vistas of the ponds below. But today we had other problems.

Monique, who was neither as fit nor as upbeat as Claudette, kept lagging behind. I noticed that while Claudette and I were swatting the black-flies that chased us at every step, Monique had given up trying to fight them off, and the mass following her was unlike anything I'd ever seen at the park. They flew in huge swarms and clung to her face by the dozens, feasting on the blood streaming down, and soon she looked like the victim in a horror movie.

Monique would often stop to rest at the worst possible spots, such as in a little dip or behind a big erratic, where the wind could provide no relief, and I would take her hand and encourage her along. As the afternoon progressed, clouds began to gather and darken menacingly, and I hurried her even more. Soon, I was covered in her blood, too. I knew I was exposing myself to a biohazard—if she had HIV or hepatitis or any number of communicable diseases, now I did, too—and that this was a violation of the park's personal protection protocol, but I didn't have any gloves with me, and I did not want to be stuck up on top of the mountain in the coming thunderstorm.

I rinsed her face a couple of times to remove the blood, which was attracting the flies, but we had to save our water for the three of us to drink, and there was no hope of a resupply.

Periodically, I would stop and ask, *Ça va?*, about the only French I knew. She would smile and nod.

We made it below the treeline of Traveler Mountain before the storm hit, and I walked the ladies back to the ranger station. The ranger on duty, an older guy no longer with the park, looked at the woman and whispered to me, "hamburger face." Neither of us had ever seen someone so ravaged by blackflies. Her face had swollen by about a third, and when we rinsed off all the blood, she looked like she had henna tattoos, so numerous were the bites. I thought Monique should go get checked out at the ER, in case she experienced any sort of allergic reaction—all the swelling around her throat made me nervous—but she elected to crawl into her tent instead. I cautioned Claudette to monitor her closely. I heard later that the pair did stop at the emergency room on their way home, and the doctors had never seen anything like it, either, treating her with a steroid.

————

"I'm looking for beaver," the woman tells Bruce and me.

We are standing in the parking lot at Daicey, discussing the water tower we're constructing on a hill up over at Kidney, when a visitor in her 30s approaches. She has a noticeable British accent, and I wonder to myself whether any beaver remain in Great Britain.

"Where can I find one?" she asks.

Bruce directs her to Barren Brook, the earlier or later in the day the better. When she heads down the hill, camera at the ready, he tells me, "We're going to replace the beaver deceiver later this week. I'm going to need you to help me bust the dam there this afternoon. The water is right up by the road and it won't hold much longer. Wait till you see this trick I have planned."

As he's leaving, he asks, "Do you have a snatch block?"

I nod.

"Bring it. I'll call you when I'm ready."

Later that morning, I head down to get firewood and gas at one of the park's service areas. We sell cedar bundles for $3, and the campers have been converting them into ash piles at an alarming rate. Nobody bothers to step into the woods around Daicey and avail themselves of all the dead and downed firewood, which they can gather for free. At Katahdin Stream and Abol, the areas around the sites are all picked clean, with nary a stick to be found. Not so much with the cabin campers. They like the prepackaged stuff.

My drive takes me past the culvert Bruce and I discussed. As I approach, I can't help but notice several cars parked along the side of the road. I automatically assume moose and slow down to have a look.

The attraction is much smaller but just as charismatic: the beaver that Bruce mentioned is swimming around, pulling clumps of branches behind him. A fat fellow about 3 feet long, he kicks right over to the edge of the road, as if he appreciates the audience, posing away. If he had a hat and a cane, he'd be dancing, and the people are delighted. I probably could charge admission. As I slide by, I notice the English woman, snapping photos. She looks over and gives me a huge grin and a wave. I can tell this little show has made her visit.

I'm glad she got to see the beaver before we go to battle with it. The roly-poly rodent is not going to like what's coming.

Every few seasons we have issues with beaver. They like to construct dams, of course, famous for hating the sound of running water. In most of the park, this is a fine pastime. Near roads in the frontcountry, however, it can be a real problem.

A couple of years ago, Charity and I spent many an afternoon up to our knees in Maynard's Marsh, pulling alder sticks and mud and leaves and assorted gunk out of the two culverts. A beaver had stuffed them so full that the road to Daicey Pond was in danger of washing out. We'd climb down with a potato rake and dig everything we could out of the way, allowing the water to flow through and regulate the depth of the marsh. And while this is a beautiful spot to spend an afternoon, looking at the astonishing skyscape of Katahdin and Barren and OJI, with rhodora flowers blossoming by the road, the standing water breeds bugs, and it's quite unpleasant in springtime. The horseflies and blackflies here are voracious, and we were each limited to the use of one arm for digging, the other employed frantically swinging around our heads in self-defense.

(Horseflies will target the hole in the back of your baseball cap. Black-flies not only use that opening to crawl up onto your scalp but also attempt to get in your nose and ears and travel down the neck of your shirt.)

That summer, every time we finally freed the culverts, we would return a few days later to find the beaver had taken issue with our work and filled them back in. This situation repeated itself at various spots across the park, including Barren Brook and the beginning of Roaring Brook Road. Beaver dammed up the outlet of Daicey Pond, too, making it almost impossible to get to my water line to prime it in the spring.

The solution was a simple bit of garden fencing around the opening of the culverts at these locations, creations called "beaver deceivers" or "beaver bafflers." We drove a handful of posts into the muck and built a semicircle of 72-inch welded steel wire in front of the drainpipe. This did the trick at Maynard's Marsh. The beaver worked diligently at trying to fill the gaps but was never able.

The beaver at Barren Brook, however, was not so easily deceived. He'd drag debris to the side of the road, climb the bank, and drop it into the wire enclosure from the opening above, filling the culverts again with primordial goo and enjoying an ever-widening swimming pool.

When we returned in the spring, Bruce decided we needed to do something about it. A friend from the U.S. Fish & Wildlife Service told him about an even more deceptive deceiver: round cages with drainpipes feeding from them through the culvert, giving the industrious rodents no openings. The park arranged to try a few. But first we needed to clear the way.

———

Bruce radios me later, as promised, and tells me to meet him at Barren Brook. The crowds have long departed, but the beaver is still there. When I arrive, park the truck, and turn on the emergency lights to slow traffic, he's swimming on the far side of the dark pool, intently working but keenly aware of our presence. He all but sits up when Bruce slides into the water in his waders.

In one hand, Bruce has a big tractor tire rim of the sort we use all across the park for firepits; in the other, he holds a coil of inch-and-a-half plastic water pipe. A length of rope is hung around his neck. I'm wondering what the hell he's thinking.

He begins to force the black plastic through the dam. "Tell me when you see it," he says, and I station myself on the other side of the road, on my belly in the dirt, head over the bank, looking back through the clogged culvert. When the plastic pipe reaches me, I let him know, and he feeds the rope through, telling me to grab it when I can. I do.

"OK, pull it through," he says, "I'll tell you when to stop."

I haul on the line hand over hand until I have a huge pile of it beside me. Bruce climbs out of the pond, looking over his shoulder to see how close the beaver has come. It's nowhere to be seen. He keeps looking.

"Duh dun duh dun," I intone, doing my best impression of the *Jaws* theme.

"I'm more afraid of you than I am of him," Bruce says, laughing.

Several years ago, working on the old beaver deceiver in this very spot, I almost took Bruce's face off when the coil of metal fencing slipped out of my hands and snapped back, slashing its teeth within inches of his nose. He likes to remind me of this.

"Back my truck up," he says, crossing the road to the little drainage on the other side, carrying the snatch block. He lashes this pulley to a stout spruce and feeds the line through it.

By this point, traffic is slowing down to watch the show. *Us*, not the beaver. We have our emergency lights on so we don't get run over, and people slow, looking for the car crash, dead animal, or other casualty. Flashing lights breed gawkers. I joke with Bruce that we should draw the outline of a body in the dirt road.

Most people drive by at a crawl but keep going. But the not-knowing is too much for one couple in a Subaru. They stop and power down the window.

"Everything OK?" a ponytailed woman asks, her brow furrowed in concern.

"It's fine for us, thanks," I say. "Not so great for him."

Another car comes up behind and they're forced to move on to avoid creating a traffic jam. The couple crane their heads around, trying to figure out the "him" I'm talking about, but the beaver is nowhere to be seen.

Dave, a veteran ranger from Kidney arrives, offering to help. With his trademark handlebar mustache and ready smile, he holds the rope as I back the truck up to it. Bruce's vehicle is filled with tools and chain saw gear and paperwork and supplies for campgrounds and an oxygen tank and rescue equipment, and I can barely see to navigate. I'm doubly careful as I slowly slide in reverse. Bruce waves me in and ties the rope to the trailer hitch on the back. It now forms a long triangle, going from the truck to the snatch block and then through the culvert under the road and into the pond, looking like the intricate rigging we use to rescue a canoe from a strainer.

"Watch this," he says, grinning. "Drive ahead, slowly, when I give you the signal."

Dave watches for traffic and then waves to Bruce. All clear.

When Bruce says, "Go ahead," I give it a little gas, pulling the line taut.

"OK, go!" he yells.

I shift into four-wheel-drive, push the accelerator down, and the truck begins to strain against the rope. I alternate looking between the rearview and the windshield, wanting to see the action but also to keep the boss' pickup on the road. The RPMs start rising, and suddenly the truck heaves forward with a great *whoosh*. The tire rim tied to the rope has ripped a hole through the beaver's handiwork, pulling a huge wad of branches, mud, and leaves through the culvert and allowing the pent-up water to flush through to the other side.

Dave and Bruce are cracking up, tickled that it worked so perfectly. This definitely beats the potato rake.

CHAPTER 15

ONE OF THE ROVERS REPORTS A VEHICLE ACCIDENT ON THE TOTE road near Kidney Pond. "Right near the turn," she says.

Tori is filling in for the usual Kidney ranger, Robin, who has a day off. The 20-something second-year ranger from Virginia asks HQ to call a wrecker and a supervisory ranger to assess the damage and write a report. When he gets to the scene, Bruce radios to confirm a tow truck is on the way and then calls me.

"Andy, can you get over here as soon as possible?" He wants me to relieve Tori and to help direct traffic so she can finish her work at Kidney Pond and go off duty. I pick up the pace on my morning chores—shoveling out firepits, making sure the outhouses have toilet paper—and then I'm on my way. I'm pretty sure I know just where the car left the road and why.

As I drive up, I see Bruce's truck with his emergency lights flashing in all directions. A small pickup, which looks to be a Toyota Tacoma, is tilted on its side in a culvert, like a sailboat heeling over, driver's side door to the blue sky. It's perilously close to dropping 3 feet into the little dry brook. The owner did a fine job packing, because the canoe and all his gear remain firmly in the bed despite the precarious angle.

Said owner, a short, bald guy with a gray handlebar mustache, paces nervously while Bruce takes down his information to file a vehicle accident report. Though he's not a fully commissioned law enforcement officer, which is typically the requirement for filling out these forms, Bruce is the senior ranger on duty, and there's nobody else around to do the paperwork. It's not the first time 54 has been directed by the state police to write an insurance report.

I drive up far enough to be seen by oncoming traffic, switch on my emergency lights, and park. Then I grab some cones out of the back of my truck to put on either side of the scene to ensure that other drivers give the truck a wide berth. The road is quiet at the moment, so I stand and chat with Tori. She's touching up the big brown Kidney Pond sign at the junction of Nesourdnahunk Tote and Kidney roads. She tells me she still has a whole campground to clean, and everyone is taking their time leaving. It's about 11:30, and everyone was supposed to be out of their sites a half hour ago, but they're moving slowly.

After Tori leaves, I step over to the vehicle's driver, who's still anxiously walking back and forth between Bruce and his truck. He says he's been fishing at Kidney Pond for a week. Originally from Millinocket, he lives in southern Maine now, but he comes up every year to chase brook trout. He was coming out of Kidney Road and jerked the wheel to avoid an oncoming bicyclist, slammed over some boulders, and found himself suspended just a few feet above the brook.

I crawl down and look at the underside of the truck. No serious damage. "I bet the wrecker can get you right out of there," I say. "These guys are artists."

I tell him about a similar situation on Daicey Pond Road a couple of years ago. An optometrist from Bangor, up for Memorial Day weekend, pulled over to make room for another vehicle, and the two passenger-side wheels of his brand-new Subaru Forester, literally days off the lot, slipped off the road. The vehicle ended up canted above a culvert. A tree maybe 3 inches in diameter, pinned up against a door, was all that kept it from going over.

"The wrecker pulled it out, and the only damage was a broken mirror," I tell this fellow. "You'll be driving home in no time." Then I add, "Besides, you're all right and so is the bicyclist."

That wasn't the case just last year, when a small SUV flipped into the very same culvert at the head of Kidney Pond Road. That vehicle dropped all the way into the brook on its roof. The driver wasn't wearing his seat belt and ended up slamming his head on the ceiling of the vehicle. Water sluiced into the SUV and he couldn't breathe. A passerby jumped into the brook and pulled him out through a window.

By the time Robin arrived on the scene that day, the driver, an older man, was standing beside the road, dripping and dazed. She could tell from his behavior—confused, answering the same question over and over—that he had a brain injury, and the duty officer called an ambulance. We learned later that the driver was flown from Millinocket to Bangor with a serious brain bleed.

"You're fine, and your truck will probably be fine," I tell the soft-spoken angler, who gives me a half smile and resumes pacing.

Vehicle accidents occur so regularly in the park that John, of John's Towing, a Millinocket wrecker service, has his own Baxter unit number. I personally see him a few times a year, and he makes plenty of trips when I'm not working or otherwise not involved.

When John arrives with his flatbed to pull the Toyota out of the ditch, he's concerned that he can only latch on to one side, and the truck is perched so precariously it might tumble deeper into the brook when tugged. He wants to get his wife to drive another wrecker in to stabilize the side while he hauls from the front. That will take another hour or more.

Gil, the park's grader operator, is in the area and hears this radio exchange. He volunteers to help. Soon his heavy yellow machine comes chugging down the road. Another Millinocket boy, Gil technically works for the Pelletier brothers, who became famous for their Discovery TV show *American Loggers*, but he's contracted to maintain the park's road. He takes up a position toward the rear of the truck, and John runs a line to the side.

At this point, Bruce and I shut down the road, stopping all traffic in either direction. Gil provides a belay, John activates his winch, and the Toyota slowly slides up and away from the edge until all four wheels are on solid ground. Success. Very little damage incurred, except maybe to the driver's pride.

———

The park's tote road, laid out for slow-moving logging trucks, is very unforgiving to passenger cars. Winding and hilly and narrow, it has no guardrails, only accommodates one and a half cars in many places, and doesn't offer much of a breakdown lane. Instead, it's lined with big rocks and even bigger trees, some of which reach out and touch the side of your vehicle. But here's the thing: it's a lovely old lane if you observe the 20-MPH speed limit.

The problem is that many people do not. We see speeders every morning, zipping as fast as they dare on their way to a Katahdin trailhead. We see speeders every afternoon, zooming up the road, excited to get their sites set up. And we see speeders every night, hastily exiting the park after a day spent climbing the mountain or angling for trout.

Our accidents come in all shapes and sizes: fancy sports cars suspended 50 feet off the road in the trees; Girl Scout vans on their sides, with boxes of cookies scattered; little Subarus several hundred feet from the curve, down in the prickers.

I've responded to a Saab that ended up on its side, having slid off the muddy road—when we have big rain events, the park road can get a skim of surface muck that's every bit as slippery as ice—and a VW convertible mired up to its rocker panels. I've responded to a Civic piloted by a very upset teenager who smacked a tree due to excessive speed and another Civic that lost an axle due to excessive rust, grinding to a halt smack in the middle of the road. A few of these occurred in the same week.

Car problems can be day killers for park rangers. By that I mean that we can easily spend five or six hours dealing with the fallout from a simple vehicle issue. Last fall, for example, a pair of young rangers found a carload of girls stranded with a flat, rain falling by the bucketful. The young women told our guys that they had no spare and needed a tow. The rangers called for a tow truck. While the wrecker was on its way, Bruce pulled up to check in. He knelt down and peered under the vehicle only to see a spare tucked up snug and dry. The driver had assumed spares were supposed to be *in* the car, and neither the passengers nor the responding rangers checked. (These days many auto manufacturers don't bother including the spare, to reduce weight and improve gas mileage. I discovered this when a van drove up and parked illegally in the Daicey campground lot and then couldn't move due to a hole in her tire.)

A couple of seasons back I was sent to check on a vehicle off the road near Nesowadnehunk Campground. I found group of college-age kids from Montreal whose VW rental had a flat. Easy enough, I thought. I've changed umpteen flats, kneeling in the dirt of the park road, hoping no one comes along and flattens me. Bruce has practically built a mobile command unit in the back of his truck for vehicle issues, complete with a cordless torque wrench for removing lug nuts. This tire, though, was more of a challenge. The vehicle had locking hubs, and we couldn't find the key. Which meant we couldn't remove the lugs and were stuck.

I radioed this in to Bruce, the evening duty officer, and we decided I would take one of the kids to the "phone booth," a series of turnouts on the park road down by Stump Pond where there was fleeting cell service, to call the rental company and find out where the key was. When we got to the spot 30 minutes later, we struggled to find service for a while, with the young woman standing in the bed of my truck. When she finally was able to hear something, she discovered that, because of the vagaries of international calling, she couldn't connect with the car agency in Montreal. Again, stymied.

Around this time, Bruce drove up, wondering why things were taking so long. He used his park-issued phone to try the call and was able to get through to the rental company. They had a bit of a language barrier to muddle through, but 54 was up to the task. We waited expectantly for the solution to our problem. Nope. The agent politely explained that they don't provide keys to locking hubs for fear of stolen tires.

Now we had a vehicle that simply needed a tire change yet was as immovable as a totaled wreck.

We looked everywhere for a similar vehicle, thinking perhaps the key was universal. It wasn't. We considered a more aggressive solution, breaking the one nut and having the kids drive home on the other four, but decided against it. We mulled fix after fix before realizing that we were going to need a wrecker for a simple flat. It would take at least a couple of hours to get one to the vehicle's location in the center of the park.

Bruce called the agent back to ask about insurance and the company's roadside-assistance policy. He was put in touch with their American affiliate . . . in Arizona.

That was a fun conversation. "We're in Maine," he told the service rep.

"Maine?" She didn't seem to know where the Pine Tree State is.

It devolved from there. They didn't have any tow trucks ready to drive across the country.

Exasperated, Bruce told me to load the members of the party into the bed of my truck and to transport them back to their site at Nesowadne-hunk Campground. We'd have to figure out a solution, but there was no reason the kids needed to sit beside the road and ruin their visit to the park. It was going to take at least a day to get the car repaired, and they should spend it sunning at Ledge Falls, hanging out alongside the stream at Nesowadnehunk Campground, and making s'mores.

The whole event took a half dozen calls and a couple of days before the Arizonans eventually discovered an affiliate in Houlton to remove the car. All for a simple flat.

CHAPTER 16

WE REBUILT THE DAICEY POND DOCK JUST A FEW YEARS AGO. OR SO it seems. It was certainly within the last decade. But there it sits, canted at an angle like a plane with one of its wings up. The decking is scarred from snowmobile skis, and the cedar boards have pulled away from the 20-foot spruce logs underneath. I find this out at my own peril, walking too close to the edge of the dock to peer into the clear depths of Daicey Pond, only to find my reverie interrupted by the sudden seesawing of a board that sends me windmilling. I don't fall in, but it's close.

I try multiple times to simply use longer screws on the decking, winding them deeper into the stringers to find some core that's strong and free from rot, but it's in vain—there isn't anything solid left. The lapping cold water, vice-grip ice, and rain through the cracks has penetrated all the way to the center of these 10-inch spruce beams. So I start to screw each of the boards into their neighbors, hoping for critical mass. Bruce suggests running two-by-fours the length of the dock, on the outside edge, to hold it together long enough for us to find the materials and replace the whole thing.

I vividly remember building this canoe launch because, like so many simple tasks at Baxter Park, it ended up as a story told at ranger gatherings. At the time, we were under the impression that the park director did not want to replace the old dock in the interest of wilderness preservation. The thinking was that a bare shoreline would look wilder than one with human constructs.

Those of us in the field, though, knew how much that dock meant to our campers. It helped new canoeists safely get into their boats. It served as the backdrop for family picture after family picture, its weathered boards aimed idyllically at Katahdin. On many occasions this wooden jetty would be jam-packed with a boisterous summer camp group on every available square inch, holding their balance just long enough to get a snapshot. On starry nights, it provided a little ramp out from underneath all the trees, and groups would lie on it to stare up into the cosmos. We rangers used it on dark evenings to scan the slopes of the mountain for headlamps.

Charity and I were convinced it had to be rebuilt, and we appealed to our supervisor at the time. He told us to quietly start gathering lumber for the project. We'd replaced the bug-infested sill logs of Cabin 9 in the same way. After years of asking for permission, we simply did it because it needed to be done. That was the plan here.

When we had all the needed materials, we set a date to remove the old dock and install the new one. It had to be completed in a single day to attract as little attention from HQ as possible. We arranged for help from nearby stations and lined up the park's 1-ton dump truck to haul what was left of the soggy old stringers to the service area burn pile near Nesowadnehunk Campground.

The day before we were to tackle the project, a camper told me he had seen smoke down past Lost Pond. I radioed this in to the chief ranger, and he told me to get my pack together and trek down to see what I could find. I did so, always happy to pull my hiking boots on. I love the trail to Lost Pond because it begins with carpets of moss that spread for acres, sitting under a forest of thin spruces with little undergrowth to impede the view. I always imagine lying down there, like Rip Van Winkle. I looked all around Lost Pond, went a couple of miles beyond it, searched its shores again on the way back, and saw no sign of a blaze. So I returned to Daicey Pond and called it in.

"Thanks, Andy," said the chief. "We're going to fly with Forestry tomorrow and we'll take a look."

Fly with Forestry. Tomorrow. That would put the chief in a helicopter not far from Daicey Pond. Hopefully, they'd come from the south and not venture over the campground, where we would be chain sawing the old dock in our bathing suits. (Please note that nylon shorts are *not* considered acceptable PPE when using a chain saw.)

But there we were when the helicopter appeared over the pond the next day, cutting the old dock into sections and winching it out of the water with our dump truck. (Only rangers who no longer work for the park were using saws, of course.) We tried to make ourselves look as small as possible in the pond, like water bugs or orange lilies. The green-and-white chopper flew several circuits, low enough to make ripples on the surface, with the chief ranger and, we found out, the park director staring down at the crew. We expected our radios to squawk with a cease-and-desist order, but it never came.

In a decade as a ranger, I'd never seen a helicopter make repetitive turns around Daicey Pond. I'd only ever spotted a few in our airspace, Katahdin as the backdrop, and those were distant, on a rescue or in search of lightning-strike smoke. Usually helicopters made a single pass, heard but not seen.

The Forest Service bird circled and finally left.

For the rest of my shift, I waited for the reprimand to come. It would be the first time I was written up. But again, nothing. Charity told me at our next shift change that the director paid a visit to Daicey Pond during her workweek to give his annual talk about deaths in the park. He arrived a little early and sat on the porch of the library, where he could not help but see the golden cedar boards of the new dock.

Never said a word, though.

This summer we have to do it all again, but we have express permission. The chief knows all about it. Bruce and I spend an afternoon leveling the cribwork in the water. Three-foot boxes made of fat, unimproved cedar, stacked in alternating directions, Lincoln Log–style, these rock-filled uprights serve as the pylons of our project. Bruce wears fishing waders, I wear a bathing suit, and we get thoroughly soaked, scrabbling on the bottom for rocks and correcting the leaning cribs with our level.

I heave upward, lifting the column with all I have while he moves rocks under the sloping corners until the bubble in our level hovers exactly in the center. It's quiet on the waterfront, and our work is interrupted only by a handful of paddlers wanting into the pond.

The next day, Bruce shows up as the sun hits its apex, casting a golden glow on the walls of Katahdin, and we move some back-breaking hemlock beams onto the library porch. They're only about 20 feet long, and we need 24-foot lengths for our new dock, so we cut a couple of spares to make extensions. We're on the deck, using the hammer drill to screw them together with 6-inch fasteners, when Robin and Laura, a 20-something probie at Nesowadnehunk, arrive to help. We all latch on to the beams and wrestle them into place. Once Bruce determines they're where we want them, we screw them together. Then we begin the quick process of laying the decking. With four of us, it doesn't take long.

We're cleaning up the job site, putting tools and unused pieces of lumber into the bed of the Daicey truck when two silver-haired fishermen stop by. They're both retirees from the National Guard in Bangor.

"Can you believe that guy was once a Black Hawk instructor pilot?" the taller fellow, Sandy, says to me, jerking his thumb at his buddy. "He looks like Grizzly Adams."

And he sort of does. In his 60s, the gentleman sports a full beard, and his gray hair curls up every which way from underneath a faded ball cap.

The pair tell us they flew many missions in Baxter Park, and Bruce asks if they knew this ranger or that one from the park's old guard. They did. The two used to haul supplies—propane, lumber, bog bridging, and whatever else was needed—into backcountry areas and then spend several days hanging out with the rangers. The park would put them up in cabins, and they could fish to their hearts' content, often sharing the boat with a ranger or two.

"We all looked forward to it," says Grizzly, whose real name is Adam. "Today, there's so much bureaucracy, pilots don't do that as much."

Sandy recalls a night when Ranger Ivan Roy, a legend at Daicey Pond in the 1980s, hosted a bunch of guardsmen. A large character, Roy heard a bear banging about in the shed near his camp and went in after it armed only with a Maglite.

"That was a good-sized bear, too, at least 250 pounds," Sandy chuckles. "And here was Ivan charging right at it. Can you imagine what it could have done to him if it had decided to turn around?"

They not only had dinner and hung out with the rangers but also helped with rescues, just as their counterparts do today. Trim, clean-shaven Sandy, who looks like the Hollywood casting of a retired Guard helicopter pilot, tells us of some of the hairy emergencies, like the time when a single-engine plane crashed into Katahdin in 1983 in an ugly storm.

"It was a new pilot, with 80 hours or so of flying time, and he decided to try and fly underneath the cloud cover," Sandy says. "He kept hitting the tops of trees and thought it was turbulence." A ranger heard the low-flying plane on a Friday night, but it was so murky nothing could be confirmed. A Soviet satellite picked up the signal from the plane's emergency transponder, which helped provide the exact coordinates. Because of the terrain, a ground rescue was out of the question. Sandy piloted a Huey up onto the ridge to pluck out the three aboard, all of whom survived. He was astonished no one was killed. "They were lucky—the worst injury was a compound leg fracture."

Plane crashes are nothing new to this area. Several aircraft have hit the mountains around Katahdin or gone down in the deep of the woods to the north, sometimes without a trace.

The most famous wreck occurred during World War II, under similar conditions to the crash Sandy responded to. In June 1944, while the world's attention was trained on a beach in Normandy, France, a C-54 transport plane, Flight 277, was carrying mail from Europe to

Washington, D.C. Onboard was a crew of six civilians on their final mission, employed by renowned billionaire Howard Hughes and working for Air Transport Command. The pilot was Roger "Rolley" Inman, who had made his name as a barnstormer with the Inman Brothers Flying Circus out of Kansas; the only military man on the flight was U.S. Army Air Forces sergeant Elbert Barnes, a 23-year-old radio operator who hitched a ride when Inman pulled into Stephenville, Newfoundland, to refuel.

The four-engine transport plane left Newfoundland on schedule that evening and returned to 4,000 feet for the final leg of its journey. It checked in with the towers at Presque Isle Air Force Base on time and on course. Shortly afterward, at 11 P.M., it transmitted its ETA to Washington via Morse code.

Then it disappeared.

The plane never checked in with air traffic controllers at Blissville, New Brunswick, as was customary. Bangor Air Force Base logged 277 as "overdue" when Inman failed to transmit his location on the way by. The aircraft was traveling through clouds and flying on an instrument flight rules plan, which meant Inman was relying on onboard navigation rather than the visuals he could see through the windshield. But that was standard procedure.

What wasn't standard was the extreme weather reported that late June evening by another Air Transport Command C-54 pilot flying the same route a little more than an hour behind 277. A violent thunderstorm aswirl with heavy winds had pushed that aircraft 40 miles off course, from the flat air corridor between Blissville and Bangor into the more mountainous interior. The navigator had to fight to keep track of the plane's location with all the electrical interference but was able to pick up a signal during a break in the clouds and correct its course.

Unsettled weather continued into the next morning, preventing any air searches for the missing plane until late in the day. When aircraft were able to get aloft, they had no luck locating any sign along the typical flight path. Boats cruised the Gulf of Maine but also found nothing.

U.S. Air Force personnel at Presque Isle suggested that the same winds that buffeted the later C-54, pushing it far north of its path, might have done the same to the lost aircraft, perhaps even sending it into the dangerous mountain region near Katahdin, where peaks loft granite ramparts well up into the 4,000-foot airspace the plane was flying.

The cargo transport remained missing for three days. Then, on the morning of June 23, a search plane, following the course plotted by Presque Isle Air Force Base, spotted the glint of wreckage in the sun atop Fort Mountain, a 3,800-footer with a long, tree-covered summit that sits to the northwest of Katahdin.

It took an eight-member army ground team a full week from the night of the crash to reach the wreckage, due to the rugged, densely wooded nature of the area. They hacked an 8-mile trail to the site from the nearest road and found the parts and pieces of the aircraft strewn along the ridge of the small mountain, hundreds of feet from the point of impact. The plane's right wing had caught on a granite ridgeline, which spun the C-54 into the peak, where it exploded into flames. None of the crew survived.

The War Department called the conditions the ground crew encountered "almost impossible," thanks to the thick scrub. Baxter Park rangers would no doubt agree. A few years ago, more than 50 rangers, wardens, and search-and-rescue volunteers were involved in a search for a lost 78-year-old from Virginia in the same area. It took three days for teams to reach John Lyon, who had left nearby Marston Trail, probably drawn by the remains of this downed C-54, which has become a bushwhacking destination. I was off duty at the time, but heard from several rangers about twisted knees, scratched body parts, and asthma attacks.

If Inman had piloted the big transport plane just a few feet to the left, 277 may well have continued on its way, with all onboard oblivious to the fact that they had flown through this wild land of skyscraping peaks.

That night, Bruce calls and asks me to look for lights on the Hunt Spur or Abol Slide. Daicey has the clearest view of these two trails of any station, and we routinely see the glowing headlamps of late hikers as they pick their way down in the dark, blinking on and off like low-lying stars. Houlton state police dispatch notified Bruce, the duty officer, about a lost hiker who called for help. It's the third 911 call today.

So, a half hour before I go off duty for the evening, I step out onto the new dock, which snaps with a high-tensile creak under my weight, and look for lights on the west side of the mountain. The flag luffs behind me, and the pines above whistle with the wind. I see lights all over, but they are distant stars, staring back at Daicey Pond with white-hot intensity. The one place not clear this evening is the upper slope of the mountain, which is covered by wispy black clouds. I can't see much of the spur or the slide, and below treeline, headlamps become more difficult to spot with all the foliage in the way.

Of course, many people climb without a light—despite a park rule requiring one—naively assuming they'll be down long before nightfall. They think they know better than we do.

I can't see anything in the murk this evening, and whenever I focus intently on the mountain, 7 miles and 4,000 feet away, my eyes play tricks on me. Undilated, they don't allow in much information. Low-lying stars wink deceptively just above the Tableland, and I occasionally mistake one for a headlamp.

This isn't unusual. I'll see lights reflecting on the pond's surface and think they're from hikers, only to look up and find out they're space debris. I'll be distracted by flashes in the trees on the pond's shore and be certain they're from illegal campers, like the two guys we nabbed in the Navy SEAL raid, but they're usually stars peering through the branches. Sometimes I do see and hear late hiking parties between the trees on the shore. But often it's my eyes playing tricks.

Whenever I spy headlamps, unmistakable headlamps, way up in the clouds, it can be difficult to pinpoint their location. They seem to flicker and move, disappear and reappear, and that makes it even harder to discern how many there are. If I call them in to a duty officer, I can sense my trailhead colleagues slumping in their chairs. They hate it when I alert the ranking ranger to hikers on high because it can mean a late night.

On this evening, I see nothing but a beautiful pond and a spectacular mountain, and I radio it in.

CHAPTER 17

LIEUTENANT TOM WARD FROM THE MAINE WARDEN SERVICE IS briefing us on techniques for coping with stress after a pair of back-to-back fatalities. We're all gathered in a circle at Katahdin Stream Day Use Area, sitting at and on picnic tables, enjoying the warm sun on a cool day. Most of us are on duty, but there are several people out of uniform, dressed, as my toddler son Gus used to say, as "simillions." Civilians or no, they're here to hear about what happened over the last few days and how to deal with it.

First was a 75-year-old journalist from Massachusetts who plummeted 50 feet off the Knife Edge in the middle of the night. An experienced climber of the mountain, he and his nephew started up Dudley Trail from Chimney Pond at 11:30 A.M. on a Tuesday, were slowed by fog, and got caught in the dark on the park's famously narrow rocky arête. They called 911 around midnight, and rangers talked the pair through sheltering in place. At that time of night, with no known injuries, it was the sensible call. The older gentleman woke and stepped off-trail to take a leak and tumbled—there simply isn't a lot of off-trail on the Knife Edge—breaking his leg and suffering internal injuries.

Rangers from Chimney hiked up and reached him at 9 A.M. the next morning. They then called for the park's sixth airlift of the season. The man and his nephew were both hypothermic when they were winched aboard the Black Hawk. The younger fellow was released from the hospital the next day, but his uncle passed away from injuries sustained in the fall.

That was Wednesday. I was at home on my usual days off.

The next day, early hikers discovered a body on the summit. It was later disclosed to be a 27-year-old male from Maryland, who likely died of exposure, although the state's chief medical examiner never released any details. Foul play was not suspected.

The Guard flew back up, this time to touch down on the Tableland and recover the body.

———

These casualties occurred under very similar conditions to the ones Justine and I encountered in our search for the missing AT hiker last season. Cold, early winter squalls in the first week of October. Dense fog. Dark of night. Light snow. This time of year, the mountain is a forbidding place, maybe even more so than it is in winter. At least in February, everyone's expecting snow and ice, the conditions are predictable, and hikers come prepared for the cold and the early onset of darkness.

An October storm resulted in the only death of a Baxter Park ranger in the line of duty. In 1963, Ranger Ralph Heath had spent a warm, pleasant day working on the Helon Taylor Trail, a 3.2-mile climb up a ridge on Katahdin's east side that deposits hikers at one end of the Knife Edge. As he returned to camp at 8:15 P.M., ready for dinner, Heath found a hiker, Helen Mower, waiting for him at the ranger station door. The 50-year-old woman told him that she and her friend Margaret Ivusic had climbed the Cathedral Trail, stopped at the summit, and made their way around the huge cirque of the Great Basin to head back down by way of the Knife Edge.

Ivusic thought she saw a quicker way down to Chimney Pond, a mistake that has happened countless times in the park over the years and has resulted in several injuries and more than one fatality. At some points, the Knife Edge Trail looks down over inclines that seem gentler and more inviting than the sheer drops for which this narrow pathway is famous. Little gullies and ravines in the 2,000-foot headwall appear to offer an easy way back to camp but are deceptive dead ends, leaving climbers on shelves where they find themselves trapped, too scared to go back up and unable to descend.

In this case, the pair argued over the safety of leaving the trail—Mower had been hiking in the mountains of the Northeast since she was 9 and thought it best to remain on the marked path. But the 55-year-old Ivusic, with just a few years of climbing experience, insisted on trying the shortcut and started picking her way down. Mower continued along the Knife Edge and eventually heard Ivusic holler that she was stuck. The younger woman said she'd go for help. Ivusic replied, "I'll see you tomorrow, I hope."

A veteran of both World War II and the Korean War, Ranger Heath, 37, climbed up that night far enough to tell Ivusic to stay put, planning on mounting a rescue as soon as the sun came up. Back in the station, he spent a few hours restless, pacing, listening to the wind pick up outside, portending a change in the weather. Heath was exhausted from a long day that included climbing the steep 1.3-mile Dudley Trail four times, but he was worried that a storm was coming. He decided at about 11 o'clock to attempt to reach Ivusic, taking with him a piton, 80 feet of rope, and supplies that he'd retrieved from the women's campsite, including food, a parka, and a sleeping bag.

Heath dropped down over the side of the Knife Edge in the dark, using the rope to get close enough to converse with the scared climber before he ran out of line. He'd need more rope and additional help to get to her, but he'd have to wait for morning for that. Although he couldn't see her, Ranger Heath got a bead on her location, which seemed to be near Waterfall Gully, a well-known climbing landmark and a place that he had gotten close to in the past without ropes. He dropped back down to Chimney Pond to get more supplies.

At 4:25 A.M. Heath radioed to park director Helon Taylor that it was snowing, telling the boss, "The sooner we get her off the better." Taylor began to scramble the resources he could find—rangers Rodney Sargent and Owen Grant, and a few game wardens—and start them on the way to provide assistance. Mower later reported that when Heath left to begin an approach to the waterfall, the storm was blowing hard and dropping an "icy rain."

By the time Sargent and Grant reached Chimney Pond, 2 inches of new snow had fallen, and blizzard conditions made it difficult to see anything on the rock face above. Sargent snowshoed to the base of the wall and tried to make voice contact with Heath or Ivusic, but the storm made it impossible. By the end of the day 18 inches of snow had fallen, and the temperature had dropped to 28 degrees. Sargent estimated that it was at least 10 degrees colder up on the headwall. Before the sun rose the following morning, the storm had deposited more than 2 feet of snow.

Neither Ivusic nor Heath was seen alive again.

The search for the pair took more than a week in "ferocious" conditions, involving rangers, wardens, several aircraft, and climbing teams from the University of Maine and Norwich University, before being called off due to snow. When winter hits Katahdin it tends to move right in, and finding anything in the great bowl of Chimney Pond becomes virtually impossible.

When spring arrived, searchers began again to look for Heath and Ivusic. In April, rangers discovered a rope dangling from the headwall. It hung above a body on a ledge encased in a coffin of ice. It was Ivusic, lying on her back. It appeared Heath was able to get her the sleeping bag and extra clothing. An autopsy revealed that the Massachusetts woman had ruptured an artery in her thigh and died from blood loss before being frozen.

Two weeks later, the snow gave up Ranger Ralph Heath, who was found about 400 feet above Ivusic. He was wearing a cotton shirt and pants and a light jacket. The doctor who performed the autopsy commented that Heath was uninjured and it looked like he had simply laid down and gone to sleep.

Every year, Baxter Park rangers attend a memorial in his honor.

I was worried that Justine and I might be undertaking a recovery rather than a rescue on that night last October. Northbound AT thru-hikers (NOBOs) are typically among the most skilled and capable hikers we see, and when one trips a personal locator beacon, it makes a ranger nervous. I was concerned he might not make it. Justine was, too. Bruce not so much. He thought the guy would be fine and wondered whether it was even worth sending the two of us up into the storm. He has educated hunches about these things and is rarely wrong.

Justine and I spent a lot of the descent zigzagging across the trail, shining our headlamps into cracks and crevices. We both slipped on wet rocks multiple times and often had to slide down ledges on our behinds. Thanks to our frozen fingers and wet rocks—and the fact that we continued our search as we made our way down—we watched the sun rise over the peak, met a bunch of hikers on the way up, and finally plopped heavily into the chairs at the Katahdin Stream Ranger Station after 7 A.M.

"You guys did a great job," Bruce told us.

I didn't feel like we'd done a great job. The hiker was still up there.

"Go get some rest," he said.

"Rest?" I asked.

"Yeah, the chief said to let you guys sleep until the afternoon—we may need you then."

This was new. On previous all-nighters we were expected to change, get something to eat, and go back on duty, taking a nap during our lunch break.

"Because we'll be searching later?" I asked.

"No, I think this is a new thing. Robin's covering for you this morning. Don't get too excited, we may be calling. I have a feeling he'll come strolling down before then, though."

I made it back to Daicey, took a quick shower, and hopped into bed, fading fast.

I woke to the radio crackling in the kitchen. I could hear the park director, which I took to be a bad thing. Usually, he doesn't get involved until things turn ugly. Then he's called on for press interviews, talking to the families, and all the difficult questions.

I rubbed my eyes, sat up, and listened carefully.

"Yeah, we got him." I recognized the voice of Dave, one of the year-rounders. "He was just walking down the trail. He's fine." Dave and Charlie, the two rangers dispatched in the morning, discovered the guy just above Katahdin Stream Falls, trotting along, happy as could be.

I really thought we would be looking at a body recovery.

We have a "Book of Death" at HQ filled with reports of all the fatalities that have occurred at the park. Perhaps these mishaps are the spirit Pamola's way of warning the hordes off the mountain. The Penobscot revered the peak—it was the tribe's most sacred place—and spread the legend of this being to keep the place to themselves.

Bruce and I once rescued a young Penobscot man who fell 30 feet onto the rocks at Katahdin Stream Falls during the Penobscot nation's annual Labor Day tribal gathering. He was leaning out over the 80-foot drop to get a picture and slipped, suffering a lot of contusions and opening his knee to the bone. I was concerned he might have some internal bleeding, but he reacted well to palpation and was able to stand upright. We bandaged his knee and walked him down with the assistance of several members of the tribe. I couldn't help but think about Pamola.

Deaths on the mountain have averaged about one a year since the park opened. Some years we have none. Some years, like this one, we have multiple. In 2017, we had four, two of which occurred during the winter. In one case, a climber slid 1,000 feet down the snow-and-ice-covered Abol Trail; in the other, a camper went into cardiac arrest on his way out of the park, having made it up the mountain during his visit. That spring, a kayaker from Millinocket drowned when he got stuck in a hydraulic—a deep hole where the water recirculates—in the run-off-swollen Nesowadnehunk Stream at the southernmost edge of the park. And in August, hikers found a backpacker dead in the middle of

Chimney Pond Trail, the result of a massive heart attack. (In an odd coincidence, he was a principal in the Connecticut school system where my sister works as a librarian.)

I can only recall a few deaths from my early days at the park. In 2004, a boulder the size of a VW Beetle let loose on Cathedral Trail, crushing a hiker. A camper died from a cardiac event at Kidney Pond on one of my off-duty days. Elbow Pond was the scene of a shotgun suicide.

Since 2017, though, we've had eight, including the three this year, and the four that year. The ten years prior to that were, thankfully, free from casualty. The stats also indicate that about a third of deaths have come from medical events—in other words, things like heart attacks and conditions people bring with them when they come.

All told, we had 38 search-and-rescue incidents this year, down from 50 the year before. This was the lowest total in the past five years, but because of circumstances, an unusual number of these involved air support. The National Guard flew four missions, the Maine Forest Service two, and LifeFlight one. More than 70 percent of these rescues occurred on Katahdin, which is typical because "Greatest Mountain" is the magnet that draws the greatest crowds.

———————

A member of the warden service's Critical Stress Management team, Lieutenant Tom Ward briefs us about making sure we get enough sleep, exercise, and water. He explains how his organization reaches out to staff after a particularly hairy incident—or a compounding number of events—to encourage wardens to talk to someone. Stress accumulates in the body, he tells us, and when it goes untreated it can build inside like a pressure cooker.

While the lieutenant is speaking, a group of angry thru-hikers arrives at Katahdin Stream's station. Tim Deetz, the Katahdin Stream ranger, quietly gets up so that he can meet them on the far side of the bridge, where they will be less likely to disturb our meeting. I keep one ear on our guest speaker and glance over at the hikers. Even from 100 yards, I can tell they're pissed—the park closed the mountain for the season a couple of days ago, after the fatalities and the arrival of snow and ice. This, of course, means they can't finish their thru-hike.

Bruce gets up to offer Tim a little backup. A wily vet, he brings over some food, which no AT hiker will refuse, and it appears to have the desired effect. I turn back to the meeting.

The warden service offers critical incident stress debriefings to wardens after they've worked a particularly gruesome scene, a case involving children, or responded to several fatalities in a row. We do the same after deaths and other difficult situations at Baxter Park, and I'm lucky enough to have had to attend only one. Several of us gathered in a circle out by Upper Togue Pond on that day to work through our feelings about the lightning strike we dealt with in August at Katahdin Stream. Sadly, the 24-year-old victim did not make it.

Though we tried for an hour, pumping on his chest, willing him to rise from the platform and hug his mom, he just lay there. Several of us, including myself, had difficulty sleeping in the aftermath. Others had a hard time coming to terms with the fact that we were unable to save him, remembering his mother's cries as she came to the realization that her son was gone. One of the rangers would leave the park because she didn't want to go through this again.

EMTs often talk of "ghosts," patients they were unable to save who haunt their thoughts. Although I often think about that unforgettable night, I'm fortunate in that it doesn't overwhelm me in this way. Rachel and I had to fetch the body bag. Bruce and I cleaned the site the next day, barely speaking. He and I spent weeks going over every step we took, performing our own after-action study to comfort ourselves that we did everything possible.

We did.

We learned later from an analysis of the AED that the patient's heart had stopped immediately when the lightning struck. He'd been seated on the edge of his lean-to with his feet in a puddle when the bolt hit the tallest thing around—an age-old birch. The current followed it down to a waterlogged tree on the ground, pointing right at this kid's site, and jumped from it to the puddle. By the time campers ran screaming to the ranger station, and Bruce grabbed the AED and raced to the scene, it was already too late. Our efforts at CPR never had any chance of working. The AED never detected an arrhythmia it could shock back into rhythm.

One ranger felt a pulse after several minutes, which gave us all a moment of hope, but it turned out to be simply an electrical reaction in the body.

That didn't stop us from continuing CPR for more than an hour. And carrying the stress of that fateful evening around for weeks and months.

––––––––––

Regardless of whether there is a fatality, we now debrief every emergency. These sessions prove invaluable for putting things in context—we often get very little follow-up information when a patient leaves the park.

The park heard from both of the women I helped this season. The Massachusetts patient with a suspected heart attack, whom we spent the night with and airlifted off the Hunt Trail, never had any cardiac issues at all but suffered from rhabdomyolysis, a condition in which the kidneys begin to shut down due to excess myoglobin. This occurs when people overexert themselves to an extreme degree. The woman from Northport whom we carried out of the Blueberry Ledges area with our backpack system had multiple fractures in her ankle.

Looking at our response to these events also, of course, shows us areas where we can improve. Bruce pushed hard for debriefs after the lightning strike fatality. He saw the power of big events to traumatize rangers as well as the power of talking about those events to inform the way we do things.

"I'll never let anyone go home right after a death again," he told me. "We're going to stay there and go through things until everyone is settled. Even if it takes all night."

A couple of weeks after Justine and I had our all-nighter last season, looking for the lost AT hiker in the October storm, a group of us gathered

for the debrief at the visitor center. On one end of this low-slung building is the bunkhouse where search-and-rescue teams are stationed when
they provide weekend coverage. A bunch of rangers sat around a picnic
table in the sun out back, with a nice view of the pond. Two of them,
Nick and Michael, were there because they had volunteered to go up
with us the night of the rescue and had returned the next morning at
Bruce's request. Justine and I were there as the principal searchers. Bruce,
of course, was the duty officer who manned the radio. Dan Rinard, the
chief ranger, attended because he'd spent the whole night in his truck
providing updates from the air force. Dave, who happened upon our guy
the next morning, was there, too.

In debriefs like this we share what happened from our individual
points of view. Each person gets an opportunity to speak uninterrupted.
Dan explained that he'd received a call from the state police dispatch
in Houlton, which had been notified by the U.S. Air Force, which had
initially picked up the distress signal from the top of the mountain.
He stayed up all night in Millinocket so he could remain in telephone
contact with the air force and receive updated coordinates. When Justine and I began our descent, he spent the next few hours trying to
rouse SAR team leaders all across the state so that they could scramble
members for a search the next morning. Dave told us that he and fellow ranger Charlie found the subject on his way down the trail with a
full pack, healthy and refreshed. The 24-year-old seemed surprised at
all the fuss.

"He'd stepped off the trail and tripped his beacon to see if a ranger
could just come by and point him in the right direction," Dave said.

We were all dumbfounded.

He expected someone to just jog up and give him his bearings? Open
a door in the side of the mountain and show him the way?

"He spent the night in his tent in a little cranny off the Tableland,"
Dave continued. "He had everything he needed."

Comfortable and cozy. Snugged up in his sleeping bag while Justine
and I stumbled around in a dark storm looking for him, and Bruce and

Dan worked through the night staying in radio contact, and the state police and the air force were standing by, and SAR teams all around Maine worked their phone trees to wake members in the wee hours. And, it turns out, rangers Nick and Michael were only half-asleep because they were tuned to the radio all night, worried about us up there.

I wanted to throttle him.

It's the same feeling I had on one of the biggest incidents I ever worked. I was one of a dozen Baxter Park rangers along with a handful of wardens, a smattering of Maine Forest Service rangers, three different search-and-rescue teams, and even a few National Park Service rangers from Acadia who carried a middle-aged diabetic man down the AT for a whole day. Ranger Betsy Dawkins sped up the trail the night before and stabilized the patient's insulin and blood sugar, and then the two sheltered in place on the Hunt Spur. I hiked up in the morning with one of the SAR teams, carrying a Stokes litter. Another rescue team had a doctor who took over care.

Volunteers and members of all these different agencies showed up over the course of the day to help carry, making long "caterpillar" lines down the trail so we could pass the litter hand over hand in places too difficult to walk two abreast with a patient between. We had to create intricate webs of rigging to lower the litter over the side of cliffs at one point, where the terrain was too vertical to walk. It was an exhausting beast of a day for a whole lot of people. I always tell myself on these grueling missions that at least we're not taking heavy fire, dodging bullets like others who wear similar uniforms and carry injured people in litters.

I happened to be on the Stokes when we got close to the parking lot. We were all excited to get back to our warm stations, to rest and eat. A ranger said, "I'll call for the ambulance."

Upon hearing this, the patient sat up and said, "I don't need any ambulance."

After a long night, hungry, tired, and sore, an exasperated ranger leaned down and growled, "We have 60 people here who say you do."

The patient got onboard. We heard later from the EMTs that he whined and complained all the way to Millinocket Hospital.

Those we rescue, of course, come in all types. Some patients are stoic and do everything possible to avoid getting into a litter. One of my favorites was a Midwestern woman we called "Sandra Bullock" for her passing resemblance to the actress. (We were all astonished to discover when filling out paperwork that the woman was in her 50s.) She had hiked miles down the Hunt Trail with a broken ankle because she didn't want to be any trouble. She returns every year and has thanked us again and again.

Some people are very gracious, sending thank-you cards and even gifts (which we can't accept). Others are not, like the German thru-hiker I went up after in a storm several years ago, the wind blowing so hard it bent the conifers over at the treeline, lifting them up at the root balls. She had lost one of her legs years before in a climbing accident—she was wearing a carpenter's harness, which let go, dropping her 100 feet onto Utah slickrock. But she was determined to finish the AT with a prosthetic. While I admired her pluck, she made a poor decision to ascend the mountain solo in a nasty squall, despite the advice of rangers, and thus ended up in trouble. And she wasn't appreciative of our help at all. In halting English, she berated us for much of the way down: we were slow, the trails were poorly marked, the park was a terrible place . . .

The AT hiker who Justine and I had spent the night looking for rubbed me the same way—and it was about to get worse.

———

After the debrief, as we drove back up into the park in a succession of trucks, we got word that 612, Robin at Kidney Pond, had been desperately radioing for help. A canoe overturned and she had four people in the pond. When it's late October, and the mountain is speckled with snow, people in the pond is bad. Very bad. We flipped on our emergency lights and tore north—me, followed by Bruce, followed by Dan. Rob Tice, one of the law enforcement rangers on duty, flew by with his sirens blasting. (You know your job's cool when it has a soundtrack.)

As I was just about to hit the Horseback, a natural esker that lifts the road up over ponds on both sides, the gate called.

"10-3," I said into the mic.

"I just got a report about two missing girls, aged 12 and 8, on the Grassy Pond Trail near your location."

"10-4. What do we know?"

"Just that they were hiking with their family and got separated. It's been a couple of hours."

"10-4." I had to make a decision as I sped up the road. I was eager to get to Kidney to help Robin, and I knew that missing parties almost always find each other. But these two were awfully young . . . I reached for the mic when the radio squawked again.

"59 to 51."

Dave asked Dan if he wanted him to see about the missing girls, and the chief thought it was a good idea. So I raced toward Kidney while Dave headed back into the park toward the Grassy Pond trailhead.

What a day.

We reached Kidney Pond to find Rob's truck parked in front of the tiny one-room ranger station. Packed inside was an extended family of Asian folks. Robin cradled a toddler wrapped in a blanket. An older man with another child sat in a rocking chair near a heater. An elderly woman was seated next to him. Robin's middle-school-age daughter, Andrea, scurried about, making sure everyone had what they needed. Rob was trying to ask questions of younger family members, fighting a serious language barrier.

The good news: everyone was out of the water. Robin had saved lives. The bad news: several of these people still had a serious cold challenge. The propane heater was going full blast, but a steady stream of kids, most of them of grade school age and not quite comprehending the seriousness of the situation, kept opening the door and letting in blasts of frigid air. Nobody was going to beat hypothermia under those conditions.

Rob finally convinced one of the men to bring a car around with its heater on. While it might have helped to have extra body heat in the tiny 11 x 11 building, Bruce decided I should head off to help with the search for the two little girls. I walked out and saw the family station wagon with the heater going strong, as requested.

But they'd left the tailgate open, releasing all the warm air to the sky.

As I hung a right at the Kidney Pond sign on my way to Grassy Pond to check in at the search, a camper sped up in a little Volkswagen and waved his hands frantically at my truck. I stopped and walked back to his vehicle, wondering *What now?*

"I just saw two little girls walking along the road a mile back that way," he told me, gesturing toward Foster Field. "They said they were lost but wouldn't get into the car with a stranger."

I thanked him, switched on my emergency lights, and called it in. "54, I have a report of two lost girls up above Foster Field. I'm heading that way."

"Right behind you," Bruce replied. Within a couple of minutes, I saw his lights in the rearview.

I met another vehicle at a turn, and we both had to slow to a near stop. I rolled down the window. "Did you happen to see a couple of little girls walking along the road?"

"Yes," said the woman. "It didn't seem right to me. They're just up the road."

I thanked her and kept on, Nesowadnehunk Stream splashing south on my left. I always enjoy driving the section of the park between Foster Field and Nesowadnehunk Campground. The old tote road sidles along the stream much of the way, passes beneath the cliffs of Doubletop, skirts the cascades at Ledge Falls, and is a moose and bear hot spot. But that day I didn't take time to gander.

In a few minutes I saw them, standing at the side of the road.

"54," I radioed, "I have eyes on."

I stepped out of the truck and said, "Hi. Are you lost?" They nodded, tears hanging on their eyelids. I explained that I was a park ranger and could take them back to their parents.

The older girl, about the age of my fourth-grade son, Leo, looked at me askance and said, "We're not supposed to take rides from strangers. And, actually, it's my aunt and uncle." She told me her name was Grace, and she was 12. Her eyes were wide behind her black-framed glasses. I told her it was definitely a good idea not to take rides from strangers, but I showed her my badge and the radio in my truck and the emergency lights. She slowly came around. Later, I had her and her sister, Anna, 8, sit on the passenger side and buckled the seat belt across them both.

Bruce drove up, his lights flashing. He said he'd take one of the girls so that they could wear their seat belts properly. This brought the suspicion back into Grace's eyes, but she nodded. Anna, a tiny thing who couldn't see over the dashboard, calmly unbuckled and hopped out.

I swung around to head for Grassy Pond, where her family was waiting. When Grace couldn't see Bruce's truck behind us, she turned to me. "Where's the other guy with my sister?"

I explained that he had to turn his truck around and would be coming up on us soon. She kept her eyes glued to the rearview.

I thought about the difference between the two searches that defined my day. On the one hand, in the debrief, we had an entitled AT hiker who was warned not to climb but decided to do so anyway, hours after cutoff. He was told he shouldn't bring a full pack up the mountain, but decided to do so anyway, and with a storm approaching. Pretty much the definition of negligent, egregiously so. On the other hand were two little girls who went skipping down the trail and got ahead of their family members, turning north when they should have waited—a couple of little Fendlers. Like Donn Fendler, the boy who triggered a famous nine-day search, they never should have separated from their party, but they were young children.

It was hugs and love and good feelings all around when Bruce and I pulled up to the Tracy Pond parking lot to deliver the girls to their family. The aunt and uncle thanked us profusely and cried in relief. Makes you feel good about your job.

We stress over and over again that hiking parties should stick together and travel only as fast as the slowest among them, but these situations occur on a daily basis. The aunt and uncle and the two girls most definitely learned their lesson. I'm not sure the thru-hiker from Ontario with the mother who berated rangers for telling him to hold off a day, questioning *our* judgment, ever did.

But it was a happy ending to a long day. Just like on *Emergency!*

CHAPTER 18

DAICEY POND IS QUIET, THE ONLY DISTURBANCE A FEW SURFACE ripples caused by the flapping feet of a solitary duck. It looks like a mallard, but it's hard to tell at this distance. All around the bird, serenity reigns. Few sounds can be heard other than the drip of melting snow and the occasional grunt of my feathered friend out there. Just as the duck has the pond to itself, I'm alone here at the campground for the first time this season—truly alone. I may be the only biped for 40 square miles, the sole member of our species for 209,000 acres.

At least I should be. Camping closed a week ago, which means we rangers can arrange our schedules pretty much as we choose, and most of the staff has gone to Millinocket. We don't have to be around after dinner to check people in or to tuck in those who are already here, so the three other rangers at Daicey and Kidney went home for the evening. The staff at Katahdin Stream and Abol and Nesowadnehunk ended their seasons a few days ago. Mine lasts a couple more weeks because it takes longer to batten down cabins, readying them for the ravages of a North Woods winter, than it does to rake tent and lean-to sites.

All the supervisory rangers are long gone, probably watching Netflix and drinking beer by now. The park shut down the mountain on October 17, about a week before the final night of camping. The park director felt that the two deaths, the snow cover, and the rime ice had put enough stress on Katahdin and its protectors for this year. Which means there shouldn't be any AT hikers in the woods across the field from my camp—but I wouldn't bet on it. We had that crew a few days ago at the debriefing. And in years past, Bruce and I have caught several illegally sneaking in to finish their hike.

The closing of Baxter Park to camping is always very abrupt and dramatic. One day I'm busy with all my regular duties, and the place is busy with campers, heading out on hiking trips, cooking breakfast on the picnic tables, putting canoes in the water. I hear people laughing on the library porch, slamming screen doors, and whacking away at a block of firewood. Day users come and go constantly, driving up the hill and poking their heads into the ranger station to ask about renting canoes. The next day, the campground is a haunted shell, doors of unoccupied cabins swinging in the breeze, life vests lying on the ground where people dropped them.

I love the stillness. Humans, even the most considerate and ecologically responsible ones, are loud. When the people and their noise depart, the critters come out of the woodlands as if to reclaim their territory. I see more moose, bears, deer, birds, beaver—all manner of fauna—after camping closes than I do all season long. Thanks to this quietude, last fall a fisher figured it was safe to stroll across the lawn between the Daicey library and ranger station. I'd never seen one of these famously shy—and vicious—weasels before. Darkly furred, it looked about as big as a good-sized house cat and took its time poking around.

Ranger Brendan Curran, who spent decades in the wild backcountry of Russell Pond, used to say that when we close the gate for the season it's the animals' park again. Governor Baxter's creation belongs to the wildlife first and foremost—that was the whole idea from the start—but they don't seem to enjoy it as much when they have to share.

I also relish these days without campers for the freedoms they bring. I imagine it must be the same liberation teachers feel on days when there are no kids about. As long as I put in my 40 hours, I can sleep in if I want. Don't have to be 10-8 at 7 A.M. to copy the weather. Some days there is no weather broadcast at all. Barring any big projects, I can arrange my day as I like—for example, getting up to work at 6 A.M. and quitting at 4 P.M.

for a hike or an end-of-season ranger get-together. I don't have to worry about providing a parking count for the gate or checking whether anglers are using fly rigs. Nobody pounds on my door in the middle of the night to tell me someone is going into a diabetic coma or their cabin is on fire.

This year we had some magnificent weather a few days after closing, and not a solitary hiker was around to enjoy it, which seems a bit of a shame. But closing the park is about the only way we can get maintenance work done. With century-old cabins, we always have a lot to do, and people don't take kindly to us climbing on their roofs and hammering when they're on vacation.

My goal in the days remaining is to cut a lot of dead snags near the library and in the day-use area. Put some clear roofing on the last green-sheathed outhouse. Finish filling my woodshed for next year. Help Bruce and the Kidney Pond rangers install a new canoe landing. And cut down a lot of the scrub that has grown up in the field near my camp. Bruce wants to use the meadow outside my window as a landing zone for Black Hawks, Forest Service helos, or LifeFlight birds in case of emergency. They've certainly been around this year.

This seems like a simple enough task, but it takes me days to first cut trees and shrubs, some of which are 12 or 15 feet tall, and then deal with the mountain of brush. Dean gives me a hand for a few hours. Filling up the park's 1-ton dump truck again and again, climbing up to pack branches down with my feet, and getting poked all over as I go definitely rank among my least favorite tasks. When I return next May, I'll have to bushhog the field to get it ready for aviation.

I think back to the spring and how cutting trees and clearing brush have bookended my year. This isn't unusual. October storms, with their heavy, wet, clinging snow, often fell trees as effectively as my chain saw. We're always clearing the road this time of year. Sometimes I feel like the park doesn't want to let us go.

I remember one such nor'easter years ago that required the evacuation of Daicey Pond. It hit on the last night of camping and swept the Nesow-adnehunk across the road, making it impassable for a day. We had to rush everyone who couldn't afford to stay a couple of unplanned nights in the park to the other side of the stream before it flooded.

Last year, Bruce, Robin, Dave, Charity, and I cut from Daicey through Matagamon Gate to the public way, moving hundreds of small spruces that had collapsed into the park road due to snow and ice. When Charity and I finished clearing all the deadfall at Daicey, there were woodpiles as high as basketball hoops stacked near our woodshed for spring disposal.

A couple of years before that, we had an even more violent storm, and many of the same characters drove up north of Nesowadnehunk Campground to remove thousands of small spruce barriers that had fallen across the park road. In some places they lay in literal walls, all tangled up well over our heads. This presented us with not only a mess but also a dangerous situation because they were all providing tension for one another, creating springpoles that snapped upward like catapults when we made a cut. We had to pick our way carefully through these coniferous knots. I took a hit to my helmet, but we made it out with all of our parts.

After I finish the LZ project I turn to the day-use outhouse, only to find Charity and Dean have stripped it and put on a new clear top. This will let the sun in and make visiting the toilet a little more pleasant. Campers raved when we made this improvement in the campground proper, allowing people to actually see what they're doing and scaring off many of the dark-loving spiders.

Several huge dead pines loom right above our new roof, however. Some are at least 3 feet in diameter at the base and long devoid of life. Bruce wants them dropped before they rain limbs onto the outhouse—or worse, a car or hiker. They are so far gone that I worry about them landing on my head as my saw vibrates their brittle boles. I had a few scary trees to handle this spring—leaners that were too far from the road to get a rope on, and one huge spruce hanging over a big drop and blocking the trail to Big Niagara Falls that I thought was either going to roll and crush me or sweep me over the edge when I was leaning out to make the final cut. I got them all down safely, but not without a lot of pacing.

It takes me an hour or so to fell these old dead giants, each crashing into the woods and away from the parking lot just as I want. Except for the last one. It cracks and spins, coming down into some hardwoods, its top pointing right at the road. By this time, it's getting dark and I don't feel comfortable cutting anymore, so I clean up and make a mental note to tell Bruce I'll take care of it before we reopen in the spring.

————————

After I finish sawing in the field, pausing to watch wet flakes the size of quarters fall from the sky, as if winter is practicing to be ready for the solstice, I head back to my camp. Nothing beats the feeling of accomplishment you get when you're working with your hands and can instantly see the result of your efforts. Except maybe returning home after a day of difficult cutting with all your parts intact.

And perhaps one other thing: coming back to a warm cabin after working all day in the snow. I love taking a hot shower, feeding my stove, having some soup, and reading a book until my eyes start to lose focus and it falls onto my chest. Days like these feel very real, very honest. Dean and Charity often invite me over, assuming I'm lonely during these rare camperless interludes, but I love this time to myself.

I came to the conclusion recently that this was perhaps my favorite part of a rescue, too. It wasn't racing to the scene, lights blazing; marching up the trail, helicopter helmets banging; or stabilizing the injured party. It was returning to the cabin after delivering the patient, hopefully in good shape, to the ambulance, and stoking the fire, drying off, and thawing out.

I realized ranger life isn't about the emergencies, the late-night Navy SEAL raids, the airlifts, the forest fires, and being Ranger Danger (54 hasn't called me Evergreen in years). It isn't about the commendations or the compliments on a well-made splint from the ER docs—all those things I imagined as a kid. It's about the life. Stopping to look at the light as it threads through the trees onto the walls of the mountain. Watching a mother mink carry her babies to a safer spot. Listening to the pines whistle and the streams burble. Noticing the ferns down by Cabin 10, which are so green they seem enthusiastic about it. Simply living in a way humans are designed to live. At least this human.

As I get ready for bed, the wind begins to wail around my camp. In the morning I wake to find a few inches of snow on the ground, enough that I have a hard time getting my two-wheel drive Silverado up the hill into the campground, spinning, fishtailing, and sliding backward. If I can't make a truck cooperate on the roads, what chance do I have of getting my car out on my final day? I once inched down Abol Hill with no brakes—"You drove down Abol with this?" the park mechanic said, holding a broken brake line—and I don't want to do so again.

I finally succeed, zigging the bed of the truck sideways up the hill, and grab my saw, helmet, and chaps off the workbench in the shop. It's quite possible I won't be able to drive out tomorrow morning because of downed trees, weighted with snow and blown over by the wind. Several rangers are due in eventually, and I don't think they'll appreciate being stuck by blowdowns—natural gates with no combinations— when they're in their personal vehicles, minus the chain saw. I have my morning plan.

I creep along, feeling the hollow in my stomach each time the tires lose their grip. I don't want to damage the truck. I don't want to get stuck without anyone else around. I don't want to fill out the paperwork or endure the ribbing from my colleagues.

I pause at the stream, taking in the view like a tourist, snapping shots with my mental camera, trying to file away memories to tide me over for the winter. Mother Nature has outdone herself here, getting the foreground and the backdrop just perfect as the Nesowadnehunk, all water, rocks, and grasses, makes a slow S turn on the way toward Doubletop. It's a study in contrasts: the white snow cover with the dark, wet rocks; the colors of the near conifers with the far clouds; the tangle of alders with the rounded lines of the mountain—an exceptional three-dimensional composition, ready for the frame.

I make it to Maynard's Marsh and slide to a stop. Nobody home today, no mama moose, no calf, no beaver. The water looks frozen enough to walk on, but I wouldn't want to try it. Clouds wrap the mountain in a fluffy gray muffler, the summit drifting in and out of view. Katahdin never looks better to me than when it's wearing its snowcap. Somehow ravines full of ice and ridges of white make it appear even taller, more majestic. But I'm glad I'm not up there today.

I move on, taking my time, feeling the wheels lose their grip at several spots near Tracy Pond, my knuckles on the steering wheel as white as the snow-covered road. No other tire tracks mar the perfect surface. I pass Katahdin Stream and notice the picnic tables leaning up against the trees to slough off snow. This time of year, with all the leaves on the ground, the mountain is visible in places it usually isn't, and I try to take in the view as I pass the turnoff for the Katahdin Stream Ranger Station.

I don't find any blowdowns until I come around a corner on Pickpole Hill, between Katahdin Stream and Abol. At the bottom of a little dip in the road, a maple arm sticks into the roadway. I park my truck at the top of the slope, afraid of not being able to stop when I get down toward the branch. After I have my chaps snapped on and my helmet dug out, Craig, the park carpenter appears and tells me the road is fine the rest of the way to the south gate.

"You headed out soon?" he asks.

"Yeah, tomorrow's my last day. I was worried I wouldn't be able to get my car down over Abol Hill."

"Oh, should be fine by tomorrow. Matt and Frank are working on it today."

Craig tells me he's headed to Kidney and then to Daicey to finish a few last jobs on Dean and Charity's half of the camp.

"How's Point Five?" he asks. "The senior of the junior rangers." I tell him Gus has started college, and he shakes his head. He remembers a little boy a decade ago, following me around with his badge on.

Craig offers me some tire chains. I decline, but he leaves them just in case, packed, as so many of our tools are, in old metal World War II ammo boxes. I toss them in the back of my truck, haul the branch out of the way, and cut it into lengths for my woodshed before turning back for Daicey.

———————

My wife always wants each season to be my last, but I just can't do it. A few years ago when I heard that two of the rangers at Chimney Pond were leaving, all I could think was that, if it were me, as soon as summer came the next year, I'd be a puddle of regret, pining for those days by the mountain, remembering the adventures as the best time of my working life. Whatever job followed would pale in comparison.

I feel the same about Daicey Pond.

In another couple of days, I'll pack up the ranger station, turn in my badge and radio, and return to my other life as a full-time free-lance writer, disappearing back into the great digital mainframe. I have enough work for the moment, but I'll have to start scrambling for more gigs after the holidays, doing the groveling part of freelancing that I hate. "You want an experienced writer for a 10,000-word project and you want to pay $650?"

This time of year is always bittersweet. As the campers depart, and the other seasonals fill out their exit paperwork, I begin to look forward to spending more time at home. I can't wait to have time with my wife uninterrupted by days of duty. I'm excited to watch my sons play soccer for their respective teams. To tune in for live Liverpool matches rather than recorded ones. (It takes some of the fun out of a game when everyone around you already knows the result and is bursting to tell you.) To romp with my skittish little 10-42, to go to the movies or a concert. Get some work done around the house. My dual life makes a lot of this ordinary stuff difficult.

I'm not complaining, though.

Many seasonals go home at the end of the year wondering whether the season gone was their last. Making a life—and a living—can be tough for those who have full-time work only half the year. For me, there's always the question of whether I'll be able to afford to continue being a freelancer and thus have the ability to return to the park. I don't usually face a shortage of work—but the getting paid part can be frustrating. Some magazines make you wait six months for a check. My mortgage is not prepared to stand by for six months.

And then there's the family issue. Every year it's a struggle. Some people may envy the ranger lifestyle, but being a seasonal worker and living in a remote place is not easy. Those who don't have another steady source of income often agonize over paying the bills six months of the year. Unhappy significant others and family members are all too common. And the staff members who are single often find courting and cavorting tricky, being away in the woods all the time.

My wife knows how much rangering means to me, and we've arrived at an uneasy compromise. I get to continue, but I have to use more vacation time, bring Leo with me when I can to give her a break from solo parenting, and schedule an escape to a warm place in the fall. At the moment, this armistice seems to be holding. But it's a very fragile peace.

On the other hand, who's to say how long I'll want to continue? The job could well change. There's been talk in recent years about adopting a model similar to the National Park Service, where rangers specialize and more duties are assigned to the year-rounders. Supervisors would handle rescuing, firefighting, and chain sawing. Seasonals would end up as interpreters at desks, and I don't have much interest in that. Even if the work doesn't change, my knees—and boss—might hold me back from rescues and hiking adventures. Bruce has already said he wants me to do more incident command training "so you'll know what goes on at the other end of the radio." I tell him I already understand all that because I'm the guy talking to the incident commander.

And how long will the park remain the wild place that it is? There's constant external pressure on Governor Baxter's creation, from the AT and the media to commercial operators and outside interest groups. Cell towers are supposedly going up just outside our boundaries. A new national monument sits to the east. Things have changed in ways Percy Baxter would have had a hard time predicting.

Our previous director threw out the rule that prohibited electronic devices in the park, for example, because people were using cell phones to navigate and call for help. (I took our prohibition on gadgets so seriously I wrote a novel longhand.) Technology is insidious, cancerous even, and always finds ways to grow in the park. Now we see hikers with earbuds, people bringing radios, campers writing on laptops at the picnic table, and parents plopping their kids down in front of screens while they cook on the camp stove. Everyone seems to have a fitness tracker, measuring their steps.

Is that the refuge from modernity that Percival Baxter intended?

It's all as uncertain as the autumn weather. So every fall, I pause as I close the door to the ranger station, and I look up at the mountain, wondering if I'll get to reopen that door in the spring.

I sure hope so.

I look out now and see the duck paddling across Daicey Pond. Will it be back next year? If it is, will I be there to see it? Every year is a question mark. Each season in Percival Baxter's gift is a gift in itself, and I'm not sure how many more I'll get.

One-season wonder and all.

ABOUT THE AUTHOR

ANDREW VIETZE is a writer and Baxter State Park ranger. He has written more than a dozen books, including *Essential Guide to Winter Recreation*, *Boon Island: A True Story of Mutiny, Shipwreck, and Cannibalism* (winner of a 2013 Independent Publisher's Book Award), and *Becoming Teddy Roosevelt: How a Maine Guide Inspired America's 26th President*. For the past two decades, he's spent six months a year as a ranger in the wilds of the Katahdin region. Find him online at andrewvietze.com.

BE OUTDOORS™

Since 1876, the Appalachian Mountain Club has channeled your enthusiasm for the outdoors into everything we do and everywhere we work to protect. We're inspired by people exploring the natural world and deepening their appreciation of it.

With AMC chapters from Maine to Washington, D.C., including groups in Boston, New York City, and Philadelphia, you can enjoy activities like hiking, paddling, cycling, and skiing, and learn new outdoor skills. We offer advice, guidebooks, maps, and unique eco-lodges and huts to inspire your next outing.

Your visits, purchases, and donations also support conservation advocacy and research, youth programming, and caring for more than 1,800 miles of trails.

Join us!
outdoors.org/join

Maine Mountain Guide, 11th Edition

Compiled and edited by Carey Michael Kish

For more than half a century, the Appalachian Mountain Club's *Maine Mountain Guide* has been hikers' and backpackers' quintessential resource for trails in Maine's spectacular mountains. Thorough trip-planning and safety information—along with full-color, GPS-rendered, pull-out maps featuring trail segment mileage—make this the trusted, comprehensive hiking guide to Maine.

$23.95 • 978-1-62842-097-5

AMC's Best Day Hikes along the Maine Coast

Carey Michael Kish

From the editor of AMC's popular *Maine Mountain Guide*, this new book leads readers on 50 hikes that can be completed in less than a day, exploring the full length of Maine's rugged coast, from the Portland area to Quoddy Head State Park, the easternmost point in the United States.

$18.95 • 978-1-934028-92-6 • ebook available

Katahdin: An Historic Journey

John W. Neff

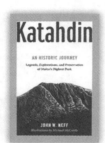

For millennia, Katahdin has loomed over the changing landscape we now call Maine's North Woods, inspiring and challenging people, from the Native Americans whose trade routes rounded its base; to Henry David Thoreau and Governor Percival P. Baxter, who forged new approaches to nature and conservation; to the hundreds of outdoorspeople who enjoy its trails and waterways each year. Superbly researched and written, this book by Maine historian John Neff draws together rare sources and takes readers on a journey through the mountain's history, legend, and legacy.

$19.95 • 978-1-929173-62-4 • ebook available

The Unlikely Thru-Hiker

Derick Lugo

Derick Lugo, a young Black man from New York City with no hiking experience, had heard of the Appalachian Trail, but he had never seriously considered attempting to hike all 2,192 miles of it. And yet, when he found himself with months of free time, he decided to give it a try. With an extremely overweight pack and a willfully can-do attitude, Lugo tackles the trail with humor, tenacity, and an unshakeable commitment to grooming that sees him from Georgia to Maine.

$19.95 • 978-1-62842-118-7 • ebook available